CONFESSIONS OF FOUR

Friends

THROUGH THICK AND THIN

"Now that we're old enough to know better..."

**Also by Gloria Gaither, Peggy Benson,
Sue Buchanan, and Joy MacKenzie**

Friends Through Thick and Thin

CONFESSIONS OF FOUR

THROUGH THICK AND THIN

"Now that we're old enough to know better..."

GLORIA GAITHER, PEGGY BENSON,
SUE BUCHANAN, JOY MACKENZIE

ILLUSTRATED BY KATHLEEN BULLOCK

ZondervanPublishingHouse
Grand Rapids, Michigan

A Division of HarperCollinsPublishers

Confessions of Four Friends through Thick and Thin
Copyright © 2001 by Gloria Gaither, Peggy Benson, Sue Buchanan, Joy MacKenzie

Requests for information should be addressed to:
ZondervanPublishingHouse
Grand Rapids, Michigan 49530

Library of Congress Cataloging-in-Publication Data

Confessions of four friends through thick and thin : now that we're old enough to know better / Gloria Gaither ... [et al.].
    p.   cm.
    ISBN 0-310-23628-2
    1. Middle aged women—Religious life.   2. Christian women—Religious life.
I. Gaither, Gloria.

BV4579.5 .C6 2001
302.3'4'082—dc21
                                            2001017661

This edition printed on acid-free paper.

Published in association with the literary agency of Alive Communications, Inc., 7680 Goddard Street, Suite 200, Colorado Springs, CO 80920.

Interior design by Melissa Elenbaas

Illustrations by Kathleen Bullock

Printed in the United States of America

---

01 02 03 04 05 06 /❖ DC/ 10 9 8 7 6 5 4 3 2 1

Contents

Confessions about ... Life-Shaping Moments

Confessions about ... Relationships

Confessions about ... Perspective

Confessions about ... Passages

Foreword

—Lois Bock

The four friends whose names appear on the cover of this book have also been my friends for more than thirty years. Our husbands came to know one another through the Christian music publishing community and almost immediately formed a bond of friendship and trust that widened to include their wives and families.

The distance that separated the Bock California home from their four homes in eastern states was amazingly small. Few business days ever passed without the men exchanging advice, inspiration, and challenge by phone, most often accompanied by a huge dose of humor; they loved trading jokes and stories. Few months went by without the families enjoying vacation time, a holiday feast, or an exchange of children—all of whom grew up experiencing the "joy" of multiple "parents" and "cousins."

Snapshots of my relationship with these four women include many fond memories.

Peggy Benson is a delightful, winsome woman and the "coolest" grandma ever to hit Nashville. She loves people—especially little ones. Peggy is the Pied Piper of Nashville, as well as of a number of other cities. It is a delight to watch children follow her. Though she is tiny in stature, she is big of heart and courage. Peggy can wear all those cute clothes that most of us dare not; Mary Englebreit would do well to use her as a model. I smile whenever I picture the lovely English garden that lines her front walk. She is an energetic talker—with a most charming southern accent. No wonder the audiences to whom she speaks feel so at home and comfortable with her.

Sue Buchanan is a tall, pretty blond who wears glamorous clothes and big earrings that look terrific on her. Her sense of fun and humor, often employed at her own expense, can break a room full of people into laughter. She has never met a stranger. Her warmth and openness make each person feel like her new best friend. She loves her business image, and the number of e-mails she produces in a day makes one wonder how she keeps those "ungodly" mile-long fingernails! She is the communications queen, the perfect hostess—the only one of us five who owns gold silver-ware—and regardless of her disclaimers about gardening, always has fresh flowers on her table. Her writing style is breezy and funny, but as soon as she has your complete attention, she'll hit you between the eyes with spiritual truth that you need to hear. In an honest and vulnerable way, she talks about her pain, her journey through illness, her disappointments in life, and her bright hope for the future.

I have always suspected that Gloria is really three people, for she does the work of three. On a typical day (which most often begins by 6 A.M.), she might be found making homemade soup and bread for 150 company employees and their families who are coming to the Gaither home for a "singing." Of course she would add a few extra gallons and loaves for needy neighbors and then be off to the women's Bible study she and her sister lead weekly. Later, on her way to the recording studio, which she will transform into a television set for next week's Homecoming taping, she stops by the store at Gaither Family Resources to be sure orders are processed and things are running smoothly. Whoops! She suddenly remembers she promised grandson Will they'd have a date at the ice cream shop after school. She's off in the hot jeep this eight-year-old automotive expert recommended for his grandmother's travel needs. This is a lady whose days never seem to stop. They do, of course, for you can often find her journaling or reading over a hot cup of coffee, or rejoicing and weeping with a friend—sharing a heart that sparkles with love.

Joy MacKenzie's name fits her. She is a joy! In her high school classroom, Shakespeare, C. S. Lewis, and English grammar come to life and learning becomes fun. All of us wish we could have had Joy as a teacher. She could (and should) write a book on organizational skills, but her joys are those of the simple life. She loves the out-of-doors and is happiest wading in an ocean tide pool, snorkeling in a peaceful cove, or shussing down a snow-covered mountain trail. Joy will quickly tell you that she is not a cook; however, some of my favorite recipes came from her. She does not delight in gourmet food, either to cook it or to eat it. She'll take it plain, thank you! One Thanksgiving eve, I remember fixing a pumpkin soufflé for dessert. It looked absolutely beautiful and received oohs and aahs as I carried it from the oven to the table. But when Joy had taken one bite, she put down her spoon and said, "Lois, do you have any vanilla ice cream?" We all agreed that the ice cream would be more satisfying, and the event has given us repeated laughs. Joy's writing and speaking, though often tempered with humor, are clearly focused on lasting values and eternal goals. Her faith is authentic; she lives it daily!

My association with these four grand ladies has often afforded me many special gifts of friendship, but none are more appreciated than those given to me in these past two years as my husband's life was suddenly and unexpectedly cut short. When I felt that my life had also come to an end, the love and care repeatedly given me through those dark days by these four dear friends helped me see that the sun will shine on my life again. Their arms of love continue to embrace me all the way to California, even if it has to be squeezed through phone lines.

In their first book, *Friends through Thick and Thin*, these four extraordinary women combined stories that traced the history and hysteria of their thirty-some-year relationship. In this second book, now that they're "old enough to know better," they draw from a deep well of spiritual resources, years of experiences, and the joys and trials of their enduring friendship to reveal what they have learned in the next exciting and challenging era of their lives. Their stories will inspire you to walk closely with God, to hope in an eternal tomorrow, and to love the Creator and all of His creation.

"Now that we're old enough to know better..."

We Know That We'll <u>Never</u> Know What We're Going to Be When We Grow Up!

—Gloria

The older I get, the more I respect children and the more grateful I am that I once was a child myself. Children know things, and we should keep them around as much as possible so we won't lose sight of what is inherently true. Unencumbered by social inhibition, they seem to be able to "cut to the chase" and zoom in on the real and the true.

They know, for instance, that new toys and fancy dresses are not good trade-offs for lap-time, telling stories, and discovery walks in the woods with someone they love. They can recognize a flatterer a mile away. Most kids have somehow come to realize that as exciting as Disneyland is, it can't compare with any of the places it mimics—the ocean, a real mountain, the jungle, or the deep dark forest. They know that holes poked in a black screen with light behind it can never inspire the same wonder as the black dome of a real night sky sparkling with a million stars.

Even today, I've yet to find a single kid who won't lose interest in television if she or he is offered the chance to make chocolate chip cookies in the kitchen, make jewelry and ornaments out of homemade cornstarch clay, or build a hut out of sticks and leaves in the corner of the backyard fence with someone who still has the sparkle of wonder in her or his eyes.

The reason we four friends find all this so important is that now that we're old enough to know better, we must confess that we are beginning to come full circle. We are discovering that the things we thought as little girls are turning out to be quite true— only now we know why!

We are recognizing that our middle years, from adolescence through the first half of adulthood, was a time of questioning, doubting, and rebellion. Trying to be accepted by our pseudosophisticated culture, we did our share of poking holes in our elders' arguments, making fun of simple solutions, and trying to act too savvy for childlike trust.

Now that, as the saying goes, we've "been there, done that," we are realizing that the most profound truths are usually the simplest principles. We are learning that there are very few things worth fighting over, and that those few things are also worth dying for.

Now that we're old enough to know better, we may be getting more intolerant of phoniness, manipulation, and pretense, and more patient with mistakes, imperfections, and even failure, as long as it's part of the pursuit of truth.

And at this stage, who cares what people think? We are getting gutsy enough to run barefoot in the rain, slide down the hillside in the snow, let someone actually hear us babble on in excitement when we find a sand dollar intact on the beach, or stop dead in our tracks in awe and wonder when we find a luna moth attached to our own screen door!

The little girls in us all have far from disappeared. In fact, we are reacquainting ourselves with the little girls we were. We are finding that whether or not we admit it, we are on most days still the same person who was scared to death she would lose her skate key in the grass and be left out of roller-skating at recess. We are the same kids who felt awkward, excited, scared, adventurous, and apprehensive.

This stage has many advantages.

- We now know that failure is not such a bad thing. It is life's greatest teacher.
- We know that we don't have to actually spend our lives doing what we majored in in college.
- We know that our real vocation is *life*. What we do at work just buys the groceries.
- We know that most people who are successful at life have "serial vocations" and that today's job is just training for tomorrow's opportunity. It's okay if at fifty we still can't wait to see what we'll do when we grow up.

As a matter of fact, we've wised up so much that none of us ever intends to grow up! We've known a few grown-ups and didn't really like them very much. And the four of us who have been friends through thick and thin have found wonderful surprises in our new perspectives. It is the *process* we are learning to trust, not the success or failure of passing stages.

So four little girls in grandmothers' bodies invite you to come over for tea in our back yard. We have some confessions to make!

Now That We're Old Enough

to Know Better . . .

Coming Full Circle

Much of life is made up of full-circle experiences—the kind of which you take little note until you are awakened by surprise at the moment the circle meets itself, and you stand there feeling very much in familiar territory and wondering why and where you have been wandering in between.

Now that I am old enough to be on that second round—or third . . . how long is a round? About fifteen to twenty years, maybe? Whatever. It's either too short or too long! Anyway, my mind often doubles back to earlier days when I took for granted things that I now appreciate as priceless treasure. It is with amusement that I retrace moments I thought belonged only to childhood and come face to face with the truth that indeed "the child is father of the man." I am so much who I was then, and I am as joyed as I am amazed to find myself so!

The teacher! I always have been and forever will be the teacher. I have just moved from dolls and bears and captive neighborhood playmates to formal classrooms with bigger books and real desks and automated systems that

21

count out the minutes and ring bells. Somewhere in the middle, I got caught up for a while in thinking that the real stuff of life is something written down by experts and labeled curriculum, and that certain practices and methods are what make the learning process happen. But I have, at last, rediscovered that what worked on the big, front-porch classroom with dolls and bears and play-mates is the guts of any successful curriculum: modeling is more effective than talking, and more is accomplished by thinking and scheming together than by hoarding answers; it is fair practice to bend arbitrary rules to accommodate relationships, and it is mandatory to toss away stuff that has no meaning for real life.

The real me is still hanging upside down in trees and jumping off Grandpa's chicken coop with an umbrella to test my flying ability. These days, she crashes and burns a lot, but it's okay, because she finds it infinitely more rewarding than the busyness of business—always doing rather than being, always putting tomorrow's dreams on hold for today's demands. She still gets giddy with the damp musk smell of the forest floor and the pungent salts of sea-side marshlands; she collects stones and leaves and bugs and shells and odd pieces of bark and driftwood, just as she used to scarf chips from her father's workshop floor to form objects or letters of the alphabet.

As a child, I heard poetry in the rhythm of the raindrops and winter winds and crashing waves and croaking frogs. I would lie under my bed, reading with a flashlight or making up stories of fantasy and faraway places as I listened to the night train that ran on the tracks at the end of our street. I learned hundreds of lines of poetry and Scripture, mostly to please Mom and win free tuition to summer camp, but in the process, I fell in love with the beauty and power and sophistication of the early-seventeenth-century language of the King James Bible. It grieves me to remember that at half circle—somewhere in my thirties, I suppose—the reader and lover of language traded those rich moments for conservation of time and energy and for keeping house and shopping and entertaining and being a room mother. I piled up books for vacation trips and read only what I needed as resources to teach or write.

Well, I still have a stack of books I am reading, but I've gotten smarter. I've discovered I can read more than one at a time—and in bits and pieces! Every now and then, I pour a box or two of treasured stones or shells onto my bedroom floor and lovingly caress the memories of beach walks and pokings about in mountain creek-beds or ocean tide pools. I am beginning to think again in rhyme and rhythm and indulge in ridiculous rounds of wordplay (which few of my adult family and friends appreciate). I've had to give up hanging from trees, but I still take imaginary journeys and dare to dream of a whole summer by a seaside. In the meantime, I sit on my back deck and lose myself in woodland sounds and gentle breezes that sing in my head songs of poetry set to nature's harmonies. I still crave those quiet times of secret under the bed, but it takes less effort and saves a lot of explaining to stay on top. I find it difficult to memorize these days, but how I cherish the hundreds of lines I learned as a child, for in most of what my mother taught me, I have discovered great truth, and it has come home to roost.

Over the years and around the circle, the necessary expandings and contractings of my various life roles have taken their toll. But today I am daring to declare that I have moved at least a few shaky steps toward growth in discriminatory skill, and I have decided not to relinquish my position as wife, mother, daughter, sister, aunt, friend, teacher, dreamer, reader, writer, explorer, and lover of language. I have determined that I shall cut back on cook, housekeeper, shopper, accountant, tax clerk, e-mail attendant, voice mail retriever—especially cook. It is impossible to ably fulfill all of these roles on any given day. Rarely can I competently attend to more than two or three simultaneously. However, I can allow them to coexist comfortably only because I know that if the moments of each day are left in the hands of a sovereign God, I can trust Him with the results—even if it includes a little cooking!

Oh! That Kind of Confessions!

A ha! You bought this book because of the word *confessions,* right? You thought, *Oh boy, this is going to be juicy!* Fooled you! Wait! Don't put it down—there could be a little juice here and there. Let me explain what we mean by confessions.

When the four of us wrote *Friends through Thick and Thin,* we thought we knew everything! At one time or another, individually and jointly, we've solved the world's problems. And we thought we'd faced pretty much everything. After all, in our group, we'd gone from perfect little lives—with perfect little homes, perfect little children, perfect little husbands with perfect little jobs, perfect little everything—to . . . eek! Where do I begin? Let's just say that, like you, dear reader, our lives keep happening and happening and happening! In the words of that famous old Gaither song, "I never promised you a rose garden." No, wait! I'd better check my sources on that particular piece of information. I'll get back to you.

It's not that Gloria, Peg, Joy, and I were naive enough to think that we'd faced every single thing in the whole world and that nothing more would come down the road to rattle our cages, but I do think perhaps we expected the Lord to look down here and see that nice, shiny new book and say, "That's one of the best I've seen in years, and being God, I understand that books are born out of life experiences, but those poor girls have been through enough for a few years. I should give them a break. They need to put on pretty dresses, glue up their hair, and go on the road for me. They'll do a terrific job of encouraging women and showing them how to love each other, and hold each other up, when life gets downright hard."

You'll see that what we're confessing here is that the Lord didn't give us a break. Oh, He let us put on the froufrou dresses and glue up the hair and go on the road and stay in fancy-schmancy hotels, but as to giving us a respite from the stuff of life, it didn't happen. You'll see that from what we've written here. You think Liz Taylor has had it bad!

We're confessing that through all this stuff, He's been right there with us, holding us up and loving us, even when we're sometimes fighting Him tooth and nail. In many ways we've learned to simplify what we know about God. We're finding out that some of the simple ideas and answers we believed as children were right all along. And we're still loving and holding each other up. And yes, fighting each other tooth and nail, hopefully not in a bad, hurtful way but in a constructive "as iron sharpens iron" manner. Hopefully we keep learning things from God, and from each other too.

As to the don'tcha-just-love-'em little girl characters illustrating this book, the four of us realized early on in the writing process that in many ways we've come full circle—we're back to being little girls again! (Can you believe that at one time we were even sophisticated ladies?) Preachers' kids Joy and Gloria, who lived life in a fishbowl and watched things happen in the church that made no sense at all, immersed themselves, perhaps for self-preservation, in literature, knowledge, and intellectual pursuits that made them the bright, intelligent women they are today. Sweet Peggy, who watched a car crush and kill her little sister and at the same time crush and kill her perfect family life, made up for the lost years the only way she knew how, by becoming a lifelong nester and nurturer. She has spent her life nourishing everyone else the way she longed to be cared for herself.

Me? I'm just a continuation of the little Pollyanna from West Virginia who lived her life only to have fun, who called herself Mrs. Vandertweezers (my little girl character depicts me well) and dressed in her mama's cast-off satin blouse that dragged on the floor, high-heeled shoes that let her toes poke out, a big hat with a veil down to there, and an overabundance of glittery jewelry, not to mention makeup! As for the ultimate final touch, around her neck she flung an animal that bit its own tail.

Mrs. Vandertweezers dressed her cat, Smokey the Pirate Don Dirk of Don Day, in doll clothes, laid him on his back in the baby buggy, and off they went up the street. Past the convent, past the Catholic school, past the Catholic church to the corner, which was as far as she was allowed to go, and back. She lived only to be known by the neighbors on her block (believe me she was!), and today, she's that same little girl. It's just that her neighborhood has gotten bigger.

Because we talk about ourselves as children in this book, comparing then with now, our editor thought it would be a good idea to tell what our families were like, what beliefs and ideas were going through our heads as children, what our joys and fears were, and how all of this played out in the women we've become today. *Sort of a psychobabble thing,* I thought, *like maybe I'm loopty-loo today because of my childhood,* but I promised to do my part. Here goes!

My father was a brave, brave warrior, and my mother was an Indian princess. We lived in a perfect Green Giant kind of valley with wild animals as friends and . . . okay, okay, that's not true, but if there's one thing I learned long ago, it's never to let the truth get in the way of a good story.

A good story! That pretty much sums up my childhood; if there were problems, and I'm sure there were, I was for the most part protected from them. We lived in a little white cottage with a front porch that had a swing and a glider. Daddy had a good job, and Mama wore starched nipped-in-at-the-waist housedresses and high-heeled shoes, and she sang along with Kate Smith when she ironed our clothes. She cooked dinner every night and made pies with meringue up to heaven. Cousins lived across the street, and we could walk to the Methodist church in the next block and to Jolly's market around the corner.

We did live in a valley: the Kanawha Valley, Charleston, West Virginia, USA. But it was a far cry from that of the giant—not a green valley but what was known as "the chemical valley," full of pollution-spewing smokestacks from the likes of Union Carbide, Monsanto, West Vaco, and Du Pont. My greatest fear in those days was that, supposedly, we were on the top ten list of places where "the bomb" (I knew about it from eavesdropping on the adults) would be dropped should war break out. That would cause the rest of the country to shut down automatically because it took chemicals to run the nation. We be would blasted to smithereens and back. Why, oh why, God, couldn't we live in Ohio? Since that was where my grandparents lived, I couldn't imagine anyplace farther from trouble in my small world.

Occasionally one of the chemical plants would have an explosion, and folks would be killed. Our house would shake so hard our teeth would rattle. Then no one would say a word. We'd just hold our breath and wait for smithereens. We wouldn't know what had happened until hours later when we'd chase down the paperboy making his way from corner to corner shouting "Extra! Extra! Read all about it!" No, we didn't have television. The first time I ever saw TV was when we were invited to someone's house to watch Princess Elizabeth's coronation. The picture was black and white—and so fuzzy you could barely make out the images—but it was impressive enough to inspire me to organize neighborhood weddings for years to come.

My own wedding, as Mrs. Vandertweezers, was to someone I called Manny. I was told not long ago by a lady who knew me then and who worked for my father in a shoe store that I talked of Manny till I was quite "a long-legged kid." Translating, I think that means I was much too old to be having an imaginary husband. She said that I came in the store one day and was asked as to Manny's well being. I got a strange look on my face, the report goes, paused for a moment, and said, "He died." She said that try as they may, they could never get me to speak of him again.

So now you know! I spent my childhood living mostly in a make-believe world with an imaginary husband—named Manny, for heaven's sake!—fearing a bomb that never came, and mooning over the coronation of a monarch whose reign has been pretty much nothing more than a tourist attraction. One other thing: somehow I understood that God was in control and that if you lived for Him, life would pretty much work out. I'm embarrassed to say I've spent most of my life trying to play God, giving Him a call only when I was desperate. If nothing else, I've come full circle to believe as I did when I was a child, that God *is* in control and that if you live your life for Him, life will work out. To His honor and glory, not mine, I might add! I think the other girls (yes, we are girls again, having been women, ladies, ma'ams, chicks, foxes, dishes, hey you's, and various other we'd-rather-not-say nomenclatures) would say the same thing.

We've also come full circle (or not!) on things like mashed potatoes, bras, books, ketchup bottles, sex, and artichokes. We're confessing here that in many ways life isn't at all what we thought it would be, but then again, in some ways it is. Now that we're old enough to know better, we know it's even okay to admit to our fears, like the fact that most days I'm still waiting for the chemical plant to blow up. Or that I'm loopty-loo for no reason at all—just because I am!

This Child Is a Mother

Looking back on my childhood is often a bittersweet experience. I have wonderful memories of my first eleven years, years which were simple and full of wild imaginings! Both of my parents loved me unconditionally; they encouraged me, included me in their lives, and allowed my imagination to flourish. They led me to believe I could be anything I could dream up, anything I chose to be.

peggy

I trusted them, and I believed what they told me. I believed in the American flag, apple pie, and motherhood. I believed what President Roosevelt said on the radio and what General Eisenhower said about the war. I saved my ration stamps like the government asked me to and respected and honored the flag, my schoolteacher, and my principal. I believed in my pastor, and even more intensely, I believed in my Sunday school teacher. From the beginning, she was my friend; in future years she would become my mentor and example. When she told me I could trust in God, for He really cared about me, I believed her. When I was a child, I trusted like a child.

29

The year I was twelve, my life changed drastically. On a cold, January morning, my little sister Joan and I were walking home from church down a hill toward our house. A car topped the hill, lost control, and hit us. My sister was killed instantly, and I was in a wheelchair for six months. My mother was forty and pregnant. The trauma was more than she could handle. She took to her bed and never really recovered. My father tried to be both parents to me and to my new little sister, who was born the next June, but he was not equipped to handle the emotional baggage of such a tragedy and eventually dulled his pain with alcohol. I know now he suffered his entire life from manic depression, which was not diagnosed until he was sixty.

In so many ways, I became an adult at the age of thirteen. Often I served as housekeeper, cook, caregiver, and especially, mother to my little sister, Bo. In my young mind were stored all those roles I had been playing as a child, everything from nurse to teacher to funeral director for neighborhood dead animals, and of course I must not forget my music career—singer and dancer on Broadway. Oh, how I loved the stage. I just knew I could be good at performing, if only I could get to New York! But first and foremost was my love for homemaking, nesting, and mothering. As my sister grew up, we spent many hours together with our wild imaginations at work. All of our pretend circumstances were much more fun than what we were living, and so we stayed in our make-believe world as much as possible.

When I think back over that time, the before and after of my life, I realize how much who I am was shaped by tragedy. I became a nurturer. When my mother took to her bed and my dad used the bottle to dull his pain, I appointed myself mother to my baby sister, and through the years, we in turn were parents to our parents as they became more needy. I was not just pretending anymore with dolls, stray cats, and Broadway show tunes on the record player. Bo grew up to be a fine, smart, trustworthy person full of fun and vitality, and she was definitely independent. I wasn't able to make a Broadway star out of her, but she did learn to be bossy! Now she even tries to tell me what to do! The beautiful person Bo became has always made me believe I must have done a few things right. If I do say so myself!

In fact, maybe it was because I thought I did such a good job with her that I decided to hang out my shingle and take on all kinds of people who needed a mother. It goes without saying that I loved mothering my own children and their friends, many of whom practically lived with us and are still part of my life. During the first ten years of our marriage, when we were pastoring, I mothered young teens and tried my best to nurture the people in our churches. During the twenty years we spent in the music business, Bob and I loved and cared for our music friends and all the families that were part of the Benson Music Company. At our home church, Bob taught the college class, and I served as official hugger, listener, and social chairman for all those sweet young kids who missed their own moms and let me love them.

It is hard to tell why tragedies come our way. I have simply made my peace with the past and have learned to see each circumstance as a gift, a way to be involved in the "life of my life," and to open myself to the pain of others, to be present where real living takes place.

If I am really honest, I suppose I must admit there is a downside to my nurturing. Some have actually accused me of being bossy! It's just that I have so much advice to give, and whether or not you want it is beside the point! I have operated on the theory that it is my God-given duty to share my knowledge and expertise with those under the caring protection of my mothering.

I must admit that as an adult, I have found myself advising God instead of praying for His advice. During the fourteen years my husband struggled with melanoma, I spent a lot of time telling God what I thought He should do to make me better at the job of being His person. Sometimes my patience with God wore pretty thin, and I was even edgy with Him. "After all, God," I reminded Him, "You gave these children to us both, and fifty-two is too young to be a widow. You need to let Bob stay well so he can help me raise them. And what about all the good he seems to be doing, all the people who depend on him, and all the places he's scheduled to speak?

What about the books he still needs to write?" In reality, instead of putting my trust in the Lord, I admit I often put my trust in my husband, a good man but a mere mortal. My faith seemed to be eclipsed by my pain and fear.

The older and wiser I become, the more I discover that only God is God. I have learned that human beings are frail creatures, including parents, teachers, pastors, the people in the church, and certainly the president! But I have also learned that I can totally trust the Source of Life and that faith is my bridge to God and to others. Now that I am old enough to "become a little child," I know there aren't many answers to life's tough questions. But there is One who knows the answer, and knowing Him not only has made a difference in my life but has made life so much less complicated. Trust . . . how sweet and how simple it is!

Build an Ark ... Uh, Grass Hut

gloria

We could work on our fortress only at recess, noon hour, and for a short time before the bell rang in the mornings. But slowly we filled in all the squares in the corner of the fence with sticks and leaves, weaving the branches in and out to cover all the holes. Across the top we wove a roof of tree limbs and a few pieces of wood we found discarded behind the school. Wild grapevine bound the framework together and helped attach the roof securely to the fence. Two cement blocks and another short board became our bench. A large rock with one flat surface served as our table. Bits of broken glass and crockery made colorful dishes. Leathery oak leaves provided small serving trays. Finally, an old rag rug mother let me bring from home thrown down over the trampled grass transformed our hideaway into a real home. A beach towel attached to the woven roof with a couple of giant safety pins hung across the opening—our front door.

Build a place to belong. Create a family of stray neighborhood kids. Make a fortress. Watch out for anyone who feels left out. Bring them home. Tuck them in. Such simple goals for life, so obvious to my "little girl" comprehension.

To this day I can't pass the right angles at the corner of a chain-link fence without the urge rising in me to make a hideout. And to this day, there is no space—hotel room, tour bus, office space, lake cottage, arena dressing room, or house—that does not inspire in me the desire to build something beautiful, something warm, something safe.

I can't remember when I didn't feel responsible. To this day I can feel the vibes in any room that tell me someone is sad or lost or lonely. When there is joy, I still can't resist the urge to dance. When there is melancholy, I feel sad. When there is a need to celebrate, I start planning the party.

I grew up in the parsonage in a tiny farming community in southern Michigan. For hours I sat in the spreading mulberry tree behind our garage and listened to the lies and exaggerations of the men who lined the wooden bench in front of Ed Smith's gas station. I roller-skated the sidewalks of our little village and delivered messages, cake plates, and just-read books from my mother to the women who went to our church.

Even when I was a little seven-year-old, Daddy took me with him in our 1949 Hudson to make calls at Leila and Community hospitals in Battle Creek or to pray for sick people in their homes. With Mother I attended every youth camp in the state and helped her arrange the art supplies for her craft classes. She took me to Christian education and missions conventions, where she always taught workshops. By the time I was twelve, I was teaching a Sunday school class of six-year-olds and planning devotions for youth meetings. Together as a family we prayed for the people whose lives intersected our own and for those far away who were also ministering on some other "field of service."

As a kid I thought Jesus was the answer for everyone and every situation. And I firmly believed that everyone else would think so too if someone could find a way to let them know about Him. I

34

didn't see a relationship with God as "religion." I thought it was just life—with Jesus as a part of the family. I knew Jesus was the reason I needed to divide up my clothes with the girl whose parents kicked her out when they found out she was pregnant. It was for His sake that Roy Dunbar was recovering at our house from a "fall from the wagon." I knew that blind Bill was staying in our spare room because giving him a place to belong was "what Jesus would do."

After I left the parsonage, I moved into the home of two professors and began to work my way through college. I devoured ideas like a hungry stray cat laps up a saucer of milk. I read philosophy, sociology, English literature, French plays, and theology. I questioned and dissected, discussed and dissented.

The next year I moved into the dorm, where I spent many nights defending the existentialists and questioning the pragmatists. I explored Darwin and Freud; I was disturbed by Sartre, thrilled by Dostoevsky, and challenged by Kierkegaard. I questioned everything, but in spite of my questioning, I felt destined to be a missionary. I wrote my doubt and my faith in academic papers, journals, letters, and poems. My junior year, while substitute-teaching in French at a local high school, I met an English teacher with a passion for music and big ideas. We were married at Christmas and together set out to change the world—or at least the kids in our classrooms.

For thirty-eight years now, I have lived, loved, written, traveled, and communicated (on good days) with this man. We have made friends with the world. Three of those friends whom we met soon after we were married co-wrote this book with me.

Somewhere along the way my life got complicated and I seldom ever visit the little town in Michigan where I eavesdropped on the farmers from atop a mulberry tree. The schoolhouse has been torn down and the hut fence is gone, but since I lived in that little town, I have traveled the world and worn many hats. Now that I'm older and wiser, I am now, more than ever, coming to believe that Jesus is the answer for everyone and every situation and that people would think so too if I could just find the right way to tell them about Him. I have found that religion is all too often a heavy bag, but a deep relationship with God lightens every load.

I have yet to meet a person—rich or poor, simple or sophisticated, educated or uneducated—who doesn't need a place to belong. And if someone is lost or lonely, hungry or homeless, sick or left out, I can't help feeling a little responsible and that I need to do what I can to somehow make a difference.

Confessions about . . .

Prayer

I Don't Know Whether to Pray or Eat a Two-Pound Box of Chocolates

—Sue

People often ask how the four of us go about writing a book together. How do we come up with a title? A theme? Do we write together, or do we write separately, then put it all together? Do we have disagreements?

In this case, Peggy came up with the "now that I'm old enough to know better" idea, and she's quite smug about it. In most cases when we have to make a decision, we each offer our ideas, discuss the possibilities, and Gloria decides! We write separately for a couple of months, then get together, read each other's material, compare notes, and try to figure out continuity. Can you imagine four women working together on a book? Especially four strong-willed, opinionated women like us?

As to disagreements, if this tells you anything, this book almost became *We're Mad at Each Other Now and Are No Longer Friends; but I Just Got Flowers from Joy, So I Think She Wants to Make Up; As for Gloria and Peggy, I Think They're Coming around to My Way of Thinking; Me, I'm Just about Perfect*. The title is long but it's not a bad idea (a little self-serving on my part, I suppose), because after the book about being mad, we could write one on reconciliation. We could fight, make up, fight, make up, and each time we'd write about it. We'd be set for life.

Sometimes our other friends (yes, we do have other friends, for heaven's sake!) suggest ideas for books. Someone said, "You should write a book about prayer. You've prayed each other through a lot of stuff, you must know a lot about it." True, we thought, at least the part about praying for each other; so we discussed it.

"You gotta be kidding," said Peggy. "I know less about prayer now than I did twenty years ago. There was a time when I thought I knew all about it; now I'm not so sure."

"The older I get, the less I know period!" chimed in Joy. "Not just about prayer but about everything!"

"I think I might be a reverse pray-er," I said. "When I pray for something, usually the opposite happens. I may as well eat a two-pound box of chocolates." Everyone laughed. I continued. (When people laugh, I continue.) "The extent of my prayer life is to get up in the morning, throw my hands in the air, look toward heaven, and say, 'Whatever, Lord, whatever!'" My friends laughed again. Except for Gloria; you could tell she was pondering.

"I've been thinking a lot about prayer recently," she said. "In fact, I've made a few notes and written some prayers."

"Well, if the truth be known, I've been *thinking* about it too. I may have even made some notes," I said. "Not because I understand it, but because I want to understand it. I'll check my files."

All writers have some sort of lightbulb-over-the-head file where they stash their ideas: half-written pieces, magazine articles with Post-its that say, "This is good, but I can do better," and church bulletins with scribbles that have nothing to do with the sermon. Files of deep thoughts and not so deep thoughts.

My file is in two parts. One is on my hard drive and the other is a drawer by my bed. Should you open that drawer, you'll find a rat's nest of scribbled-on scraps torn from what have you: magazines, airline tickets, paper napkins, you name it. Don't bother trying to decipher them; I barely can. They were written in the night, in the dark, or on the run.

"I'm sure I have notes too," said Joy.

39

"We don't have to have all the answers," Peggy agreed. "We'll just confess it right up front, and then maybe our readers will simply join us on our journey. Let's all go home and see what we have on the subject."

Sure enough, when I checked, I found a computer file on prayer. There were three entries. One was a prayer titled "Johnny on the Spot." Here are the other two:

Sue's Silent Prayers (followed by several blank pages)
Sue's Unspoken Requests (followed by several blank pages)

It didn't take me long to realize that my prayers weren't ready for prime time, but as Peggy said, "Maybe our readers would simply like to join us on our journey."

With that in mind, work your way through this first section of our book. Discover that Joy's prayer closet isn't really a closet after all. Meet Peggy's Brother Browning, the wise old saint who taught her a thing or two about the subject. Find out my unorthodox spot for praying, and share in Gloria's intimate moments with the Father, remembering she had a head start on the rest of us.

The theme for this section could have just as well been named "Prayer as It Relates to Our Children," because several of our offerings take that turn. I especially enjoyed telling the joyous and romantic love story (at least a tiny bit of it) of my daughter Dana and son-in-law Barry and how I survived what is commonly called bloody tongue syndrome. Enjoy!

Sometimes I Can't Sleep, Lord

—Gloria

Sometimes I can't sleep, Lord.
At night everything looms large before my
   mind.
At night the issues of the day organize
      themselves into an army,
         marching like an enemy battling
            to pillage my storehouse of peace.
Worries and concerns of the day turn into
      terrors of the night.
Simple shortcomings and human frailties
      become terminal failures for which
         there is no grace or mercy.
I feel as if I am slipping off a precipice
      and the sapling I grasp
         is coming up by the roots.
I am alone and a stalker
      lurches in the shadows.
I know, Lord, that You are not
      the author of confusion.
You are never the source of fear,
      for fear is the opposite of faith;
I recognize the terror of the night
      as the imposition of Satan.

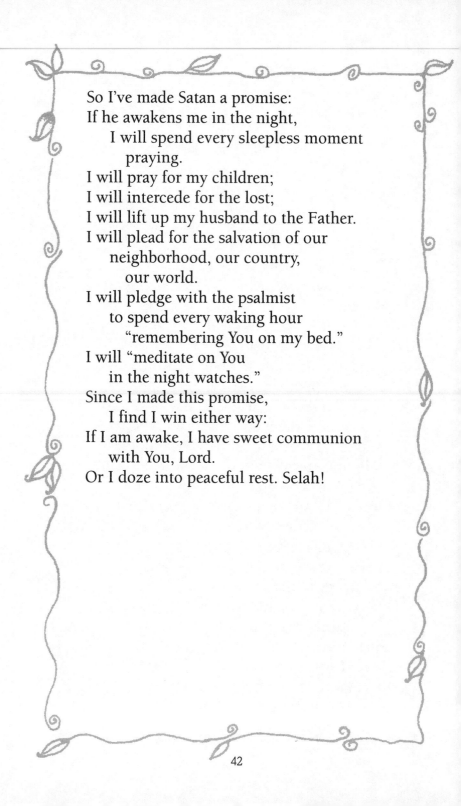

So I've made Satan a promise:
If he awakens me in the night,
    I will spend every sleepless moment
      praying.
I will pray for my children;
I will intercede for the lost;
I will lift up my husband to the Father.
I will plead for the salvation of our
    neighborhood, our country,
      our world.
I will pledge with the psalmist
    to spend every waking hour
      "remembering You on my bed."
I will "meditate on You
    in the night watches."
Since I made this promise,
    I find I win either way:
If I am awake, I have sweet communion
    with You, Lord.
Or I doze into peaceful rest. Selah!

Prayer on Wheels

These days, everything seems to be going mobile. My prayer closet is no exception. Though I knew, even as a child, that God can be addressed from any point on (or off) the planet, prayer took place more comfortably for me in a church pew, beside a bed, or at least in a quiet place. Emergencies excepted, these were normally the places in which I had conversations with God . . . until I had children!

If a prayer closet once existed in a house now inhabited by toddlers and teenagers, it had probably relinquished its space to an assortment of off-season clothing, a collection of single mittens, a one-eyed teddy bear, a bald-headed Barbie, and a melange of miscellaneous athletic gear. If God needed a quiet place to communicate, He had left the building.

I don't remember exactly on what occasion I made the discovery—I suppose it was a natural progression born of necessity—but sometime during the years when my house was rocking with activity, my car became my customary place of prayer. (So much for "every head bowed, every eye closed!") It has turned out to be quite an appropriate environment—a soundproof place in which I can sing aloud, praise, plead, beg, scream, cry, complain, or converse reasonably without interruption as my invisible partner is capable of both listening and maneuvering us through danger when my eyes are too blinded by passion or tears. (And to think how I used to roll my eyes at those bumper stickers that said, "God is my copilot!") Believe me, on most days, a moving prayer closet needs a copilot!

Strangely enough, my mobile unit has also been a place quiet enough to accommodate a still small voice speaking into my life words of sanity, refreshment, reproof, and wisdom. On school days, it is the place in which my schedule gets ordered for the day. I can almost feel the computer chips rearrange themselves in my head as I ask that His agenda replace mine. (I'm learning . . . if slowly. I've tried the plans I create all by myself!) I ask to be reminded of things that will become important on that day, especially people who may need His touch through me. (Yes, finally, I am able to admit that I'm far too self-absorbed to figure that out alone.)

The car is also the place I have learned to adopt an attitude of open-handedness toward all those belea-guering, unsolvable problems of my busy life—the stuff that never seems to go away, no matter how hard I pray or how much I worry or how patient I think I am or how many times I "remind" God about my need for resolution.

Ha! Maybe the lesson is in the car. Driving a car is a good metaphor for such a misguided life. When I'm behind the wheel, I think I'm in charge of this vehicle. But I'm forgetting a few very important things: I didn't make this piece of machinery, I am powerless to control all the elements that move around it, and I can't begin to suspect what nasty little devils inside its workings will raise their evil heads at any given moment and stop me cold.

As it turns out, a car is a perfect reminder that God is in control. If He can be trusted to safely guide the course of a driver who can barely manage a steering wheel and conversation at the same time, surely He is qualified to choose the setting and the subject matter of my prayer time. How easy it is, then, to believe that His responses to my needs will be both faithful and wise!

Prayer and Peanut Butter

The family across the street was vegetarian Seventh Day Adventist. Linda was just my age, and her toddler brother, David, was about five years younger. She cared for him most of the day while her mother did housework or cooked. Their house always had the aroma of peanut butter and soybeans because these two foods were the family's main source of protein, and from these all sorts of menu items were invented. My memory is that their house was also relatively dark because they were extremely frugal people and saved money any way they could, including eliminating the unnecessary use of electricity. They gave a large portion of their small income to "the missionaries," as Linda often told me, and ate fish and chicken only when it was given to them.

Most of the day, Linda and David played outside in their yard, or in ours when I would call across the street, "Can you come over?" Linda

gloria

would "check with her mother," then pull her brother in her worn-out once-red wagon across the street and park him in the shade of the big maples growing in our yard. A peeled carrot, a few crackers, and his bottle of soymilk and he was a happy camper.

Two days of the week I seldom saw my friend: Saturdays and Sundays. Since my parents were pastors of a small but active village church, our Sundays were packed with two services, Sunday school, youth meetings, and Sunday dinner with one or more church families. For Linda, from sundown Friday to sundown Saturday, her family strictly observed the Sabbath. That meant no playing with friends across the street or any other frivolous activity.

Our church youth group practically lived at our house. I sometimes wondered what Linda thought as teenagers ran in and out of the parsonage after school or ballgames and came to talk to my mother who was their friend, confidant, and counselor. In the spring and summer, Mother would take us all fishing or hiking up Dixon Hill, where my father would meet us with our old Hudson sedan fully loaded with all the provisions for a hotdog roast and bonfire. We would fill our growling stomachs with hotdogs and s'mores and sing sweet choruses around the campfire long into the starry Michigan nights to the accompaniments of crickets, cicadas, and the simple guitar chords played by Ray Funk's dad, George. In the winter, my mother would organize snow-sledding parties and bring apple cider and hot chocolate to warm in blue splatterware enamel coffeepots over the open fire. We would sing Christmas songs and camp tunes while we thawed our frostbitten fingers over the orange flames.

One summer night, the youth group was having a huge party in our back yard. The volleyball net was stretched across the yard behind the garage. Croquet was set up near the flower garden. Daddy had a huge bonfire laid at the end of the driveway. Many of the moms had fixed potato salad, baked beans, cream-cheese-and-olive-stuffed celery stalks, fresh fruit, and chocolate brownies. Watermelon and hotdogs were a given!

All the laughter and games, the singing, and the bonfire attracted Linda and little David as they played on the swing beside their screened-in porch. I saw them and motioned for Linda to join us. She disappeared into the house, then returned with a triumphant grin spread across her freckled face. Rarely did her mother allow her to come when there was any church activity going on, perhaps fearing some attempt at proselytizing by our parishioners.

What a night we all had—playing hard, then gathering around the fire, roasting hotdogs on long sticks I'd helped Daddy sharpen with our pocketknives. Linda and David held back from the food table and the fire. They had been taught to be careful of "foreign" food and unfriendly prejudice against their "different" lifestyle.

Linda was pulled into the circle by one caring teenager, and timidly she accepted a brownie. I saw David sitting in his wagon and decided it would be funny to see how he would react to the taste of a hotdog. I broke off a bite-sized piece and offered it to him. Sure enough, he licked his little lips and begged for more. What I did not know, however, was that my mother had walked up behind me and had seen what I was up to.

"Gloria!" I knew the tone in her voice. She took my arm and pulled me into the dark where she could talk.

"Don't you ever let me catch you violating the innocent trust of a child again," she said. "We may not share all of that family's beliefs, but we *will* respect them, and until David is old enough to choose for himself, we must protect what they believe is right for him. You must never do anything to cause anyone of any religion to violate his or her own conscience."

It was a lesson I would never forget and one I needed to learn early. Child as I was myself, my friend's dietary laws seemed strange and humorous to me. My narrow view was that whatever our family did was the right way. Anything else was either wrong or unnecessary.

I now have a friend whose husband is dying of pancreatic cancer. He has never been a religious man, but she has been a devout Catholic all her life. She is one of the most committed Christians I know and has given herself for the cause of Christ in more ways than I can count. Servanthood is a way of life for her.

Not long ago her husband asked her to call the priest from our small-town Catholic church to come to the house. He had decided he wanted to give his life to God in a real way, not just accept the final rites when his time came to die.

Nesie went to buy him his first rosary and to ask a few close friends if they would come to share in his decision and confirmation. It was a moment for which she had prayed her whole married life.

A few weeks earlier Bill and I were in Rome. We were thrilled to see some of the greatest art of all time, such as Michelangelo's two *Pietas*, his *David*, and the glorious ceiling of the Sistine Chapel. We also visited the Colosseum, where many Christians were devoured by lions, the dungeon where Paul and Silas were chained and imprisoned, and the Forum. We toured St. Peter's and the Vatican.

Among all the magnificent sites, one little church that was once the home of a wealthy early Christian seemed to beckon me inside. We learned that many first-century Christians were buried under this building and that the original owners shared their home as a meeting place and a hiding place for the early believers of Rome. Today this is a church that specializes in ministering to the street people, the addicts, and the poor.

I slipped away from the friends who shared our trip to kneel in this quiet place. A stream of sunshine was cutting a golden diagonal across the sanctuary from a simple amber stained-glass window. I knelt there and prayed for Nesie and for her husband, the new Christian. I am Protestant, but I needed to pray *there* for her. I wanted to tell her how I've prayed for them both in other places, but this prayer in this sanctuary was a gift my mother taught me long ago to give.

"What are you doing?" Bill asked when I came out of the church.

Eating peanut butter and soybeans, I thought, *and being thankful.*

"Just praying," I said.

My Secret Sanctuary

When I was a child, I thought prayer was just for old people. I suppose I assumed that it was something for them to do in their December years to keep them busy. But it wasn't long before I realized that the people I felt drawn to, whether young or old, were those who seemed to know God personally, who prayed and spoke of prayer as if they knew some big secret. Since I love secrets, I was just curious enough to need to know what they had that I didn't, so I began to pay attention. Oh, the discoveries I made!

The first real prayer warrior in my life was not my mother or father but someone who gave my parents strength and courage and hope. They came to know the Lord through Raymond Browning, a minister from North Carolina, where my parents lived when I was born. Mom and Dad always looked to him for counsel, and any time he was in the Nashville area, he had a bedroom at our house. As a little girl, I could hardly wait for him to come.

Brother Browning looked like what I envisioned God might look like. He was a tall, handsome man with snow-

peggy

white hair that ended in soft curls above his shirt collar. He was always immaculately dressed in a suit and tie, complete with a vest and a gold pocket watch. I can remember looking out my window and seeing him walking in the back yard, waiting for my folks to call him in for breakfast. He would talk and gesture in the air as he walked. Sometimes he would throw back his head and laugh.

Once, I ran downstairs and out the back door and interrupted him to ask who he was talking to so loudly. He told me that he spoke his prayers in the morning to the Heavenly Father in a loud voice of grateful praise. I said I thought praying was what church was for, and he helped me begin to understand that church was only a very small part of the life of prayer, that there was a sacred place, a sanctuary, deep inside me where I could meet God and talk to Him, on my own, anytime I wanted. He reminded me that since I had asked the Lord to live in my heart, I could make my very own house of prayer.

So the secret began to unfold. Since I was an only child for a long time and was often lonely, I spent a lot of time making playhouses in closets and tent homes under trees and talking to myself. The thought of having my very own friend to listen to me and to talk to me in my own home sounded inviting!

As I got older and began to develop my own faith, I began to understand what those old prayer warriors had discovered so long ago. Prayer doesn't require that the pray-er do all the talking! It actually involves a great deal of listening. Listening involves a lot of work for me, since I am such a talker! When I get down to it, there isn't much I have to say to God that He hasn't heard before. It is not so much that God needs my prayers or instructions or suggestions; it's more that I need to hear what He might be trying to say to me. What a blessing there is in learning to be still and know Him. So half of getting to own the secret is to discipline myself to be still—tough stuff for me! The word *discipline* is not one of my favorites. And I really don't care for the word *shh* either. Somehow it brings out the talk in me!

So I keep asking myself this question: If God should speak to me in a whisper, is there ever a time in my day when I am quiet enough to hear Him?

> Take my yoke upon you and learn from me . . . and you will find rest for your souls.
>
> —MATTHEW 11:29

> I heard the voice of Jesus say, "Come unto Me and rest;
> Lay down, thou weary one, lay down Thy head upon My
>   breast."
> I came to Jesus as I was, weary, and worn, and sad;
> I found in Him a resting place, and He has made me glad.
> I heard the voice of Jesus say, "Behold, I freely give
> the living water; thirsty one, stoop down, and drink and live."
> I came to Jesus and I drank of that life-giving stream;
> My thirst was quenched, my soul revived, and now I live in
>   Him.
> I heard the voice of Jesus say, "I am this dark world's light;
> Look unto Me, thy morn shall rise, and all the day be bright."
> I looked to Jesus, and I found in Him my star, my sun;
> And in that Light of life I'll walk, till trav'ling days are done.
>
> —HORATIUS BONAR,
> "I HEARD THE VOICE OF JESUS SAY"

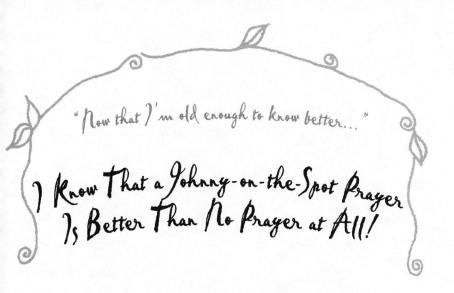

I Know That a Johnny-on-the-Spot Prayer Is Better Than No Prayer at All!

I've broken many a fingernail digging like a mad woman through purses and briefcases for chocolate. I've frantically scratched around in drawers or in the backs of cabinets, searching for even a single renegade chocolate chip. One with mold will do, for heaven's sake! When it comes to chocolate, I can be a desperate woman.

While searching my briefcase, I'm liable to find most anything: a letter or note someone has hidden there, a table favor from a luncheon where I've spoken, business cards of folks I want to keep in touch with, expense reports, notes to myself, and even book ideas. Not long ago, during a desperate chocolate search, I found this poem on the back of an envelope. I have no idea when or where I wrote it, but apparently it was on the go:

Here I am again, Lord;
It's me!
Speaking to You from a toilet stall.
It seems we've had some of our best talks here.
From my point of view

It's a place to talk to You privately.
From Your point of view
You're probably just glad to hear from me.
Sometimes I ignore You for days on end.
Then, in a toilet stall, I'm begging You for immediate action.
"Let me not throw up from fright."
"Help it all go smoothly."
The most important thing I've learned about You
Is that You are there
When I need You.
Whenever! Wherever!

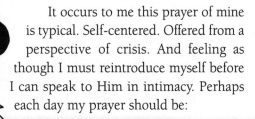

It occurs to me this prayer of mine is typical. Self-centered. Offered from a perspective of crisis. And feeling as though I must reintroduce myself before I can speak to Him in intimacy. Perhaps each day my prayer should be:

It's not about me, dear God,
It's about You.
Let me know You.

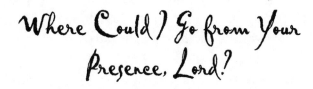

Where Could I Go from Your Presence, Lord?

—Gloria

Where could I go from Your presence, Lord?"
    is more than a rhetorical question these
        days.
Where my journey has taken me
    has been something I could never have
        plotted or planned.
No road club could have printed out maps
    for this trip.
Yet I never left the palm of Your hand.
Now, more than ever, I am at rest
    in Your sweet embrace.
How can this be?
Turbulent times should be unsettling.
Strange territory should leave us
    feeling bewildered and disoriented.
Yet here I am—somehow at rest
    in Your presence.
This rest is familiar, reassuring, peaceful.
The psalmist must have learned this, too.
I can never be lost from Your presence.

If I go down to hell, Your presence
    surrounds me like a safe harbor.
If I fly through the heavens
    on the wings of the morning,
        Your sweet presence
            puts Music to the Words.
You are the eye of the storm.
You are the cleft in the rock.
You are the whale in the bottom of the sea.
I've never been here before, Lord,
    but I know where I am.
I am with You.

I Don't Want to Be the Most Significant Influence in My Children's Lives

When my mother was dying, I suddenly realized that without her, I would no longer have access to several of the great secrets of the universe—like her recipe for Christmas cut-out sugar cookies and a special rice dish that was a family favorite. I had no idea how she got the tapioca pudding that everyone else seemed to make the consistency of wallpaper paste to be so light and fluffy. And there were all her versions of Florentine Tititian, which it took me until teenage years to realize were various concoctions of her own imagination, created by the necessity of entertaining guests out of the paucity of a poor, small-town preacher's larder. She thought it clever wordplay to dub the capricious cuisine, which was never twice the same, a foreign-sounding modification of her name, Florence Titus. It was her little secret, which eventually became the family's, and one we much enjoyed. I fully intended to emulate the practice when I grew up and entertained strangers, but I was never able to derive from Joy MacKenzie any adjective-noun combination that sounded sophisticated enough. (My "friends" would probably think the label *Mediocre au Joi* appropriate!) Given my lack of interest in cooking, I'd just as soon credit any dish I create to someone else.

Mother was a woman for whom life was an adventure, and she brought to our days of growing up in the parsonage a spirited flexibility uncommon to the household of a midcentury Baptist preacher. Her style was vivacious and direct. Her expressions of joy and frustration, approval and reproof were all full steam ahead. She was not the soft, cuddly, fold-you-in-her-arms type, but her heart was as wide with compassion as were the doors of her house. We were never allowed to have cats or dogs (which she deemed "germy"), but our modest manse was open to strays, misfits, missionaries, kids out of kilter with their parents, and parents who couldn't get along with each other. Mother would cry with all of them (and with us), but there was always closure to the commiserating—a solution of sorts, most often framed by phrases such as, "This is real life! It's too short to go on bellyaching."

She was the exchequer of chicanery, instigating all sorts of bizarre jokes and tricks on everybody from the rather stern chairman of the board of deacons to the choleric old lady who sat, every Sunday, in exactly the same balcony seat, from which she critiqued the misbehavior of the teenagers below. This crazy Baptist preacher's wife hosted such unheard of events as a coed slumber party for the church youth group, at which she led the escape of the girls from a second-floor window to surprise, with a garden hose shower, the boys who were trying to sneak into the second floor from the garage roof. Then she taunted my father for being a slacker on his first-floor watch. She helped us make up silly poems about parishioners who criticized or provoked us, and we were allowed to vent freely (and privately) our frustrations at living a goldfish-bowl life. But when it came to spiritual matters, she was straightforward, no-nonsense, drop-dead serious.

Her "motherly" inscription in the Bible she and Dad gave me upon my graduation from junior high school said, "This book will keep you from sin; sin will keep you from this book." "Be sure your sin will find you out" was often a last reminder as I left the house on a date. Mother believed that memorizing Scripture and other literature of beauty and truth was a vanguard against evil, and she saw to it that by the time we left home for college, we were armed, not only with truth but with a love for words and an understanding of their power. Shakespearean sonnets, Psalms, Proverbs, and silly rhymes were served to us like supper. It was one of her greatest gifts to her children.

So as I began to deal with the reality of not having this treasure much longer, I suddenly realized that she possessed some wisdom that I was desperate to hold on to. My children were six and three at the time, and she was not going to be available for motherly advice in their teenage years. She knew stuff about raising kids that I was afraid I wouldn't discover on my own. So I asked her how she managed to survive all the crises of the teenage years. After all, she had raised four children who, as adults, were still whole and wholly connected to her God. "Please, Mom," I begged. "Tell me the important things I'm going to need to know."

I'll never forget her answer.

"Do whatever it takes to keep the communication lines open. Keep talking to them. But more importantly, keep talking to God about them. Teach them God's Word. You will discover that truth which has been planted in their hearts in early years gets a better chance of being heard than any words a parent can speak."

So this funny, outlandish tower of strength, model that she was, was not enough. Florentine Tititian she could concoct on her own, but when it came to the spiritual lives of her children, all she could do was to talk to them, fill them with truth, and pray for them.

I have tried to love my children well. I have talked to them more than they would have wished (in spite of which we're still talking, twenty-some years later). I have taught them Scripture and poetry and filled their heads and their shelves with good literature. But the wisdom of my mother's advice has often drawn me to prayer, and I have to say that in the final analysis, it is an incredibly reassuring act for a mother to engage in conversation with a God who, at any given moment, is absolutely tuned to every nuance of her children's current thoughts and deeds.

It's nice to be intimately acquainted with someone who has a more positive and powerful influence in my children's lives than I do!

I've Discovered the Benefits of Biting My Tongue When It Comes to My Kids

(Ouch, Ooo, Yowl!)

From the time Dana was born, we prayed that she would someday marry the right person and that it would be God's choice, not ours. It took Dana a long time to show even the slightest interest in boys. She was a late bloomer. By the time she was in the eleventh grade, we'd pretty much pegged her as antisocial and slightly boring. Yes, I know she is my very own daughter and that's a cruel thing to say, but sometimes a mother has to face facts.

Then in her senior year, she discovered the harp, and suddenly she was known; she was in demand to play at every event: talent shows and musicals—she even became a member of the Nashville Youth Symphony. One night when she returned from a rehearsal—we always waited up to help her unload, lamenting the fact she hadn't chosen to play piccolo— she had with her the cutest, tallest, most muscular, blond-haired boy you ever laid eyes on. Balanced on one shoulder was the harp. Heretofore, it took the three of us to manipulate it out of the station wagon, into the house, and up the stairs. *Whoosh,* went the wind out of Wayne's sails when he realized he might never be needed again. If for no other reason than that, we knew this boy couldn't possibly be the one.

After the blond Adonis came a total opposite: a dark, fun-loving Jewish boy, and we all fell in love, especially Wayne after he discovered David couldn't move the harp by himself. My guess is, knowing David, that even if he could have, he was smart enough to play the game.

It wasn't unusual for Dana and David to come home late after a date and barge right in to our room ready to entertain us with their evening's adventures. It was fun while it lasted. We knew down deep David wasn't the one; his background was very Jewish, and Dana's was very Christian. Each recognized that their heritage was part of who they were, and neither intended to change.

In college Dana met Barry, and it didn't take long for us to figure out this was the one! Watching the two of them together was like watching six-year-olds who simply took delight in each other's presence. Barry's parents, Bonnie and Miles, whom we'd met and fallen in love with, were having the same thoughts we were: these two were meant for each other. In our minds, Bonnie and I were planning a wedding. We chose the colors for our dresses, for heaven's sake!

The problem was that Dana and Barry didn't cooperate! Dana assured us they could never date; they were best friends. "Almost like brothers and sisters," she said. They graduated from college with no wedding in sight.

Every year, Dana and Barry and their other best friends, Deba and Cary (also not a couple), took a vacation together. Throughout the year, they would visit each other: Barry would come to Nashville, or she would go to Middletown, Ohio. They dated other people, and if he broke up with someone, she was by his side, comforting him. If she broke up with someone, Barry was there, hugging, patting, consoling.

Looked like love to me, but what do I know? I'm just the mother.

Once when I was planning a business trip to Columbus, Ohio, Dana insisted that instead of flying I should drive so she could go with me. The plan would be to drop her off in Middletown on the way and pick her up on the way back. Things went according to plan. I dropped her off, continued to Columbus for a couple of days, did my work, and returned to the designated meeting place in Middletown: the Bob Evans restaurant. They were there, and I pulled in next to them. And I waited. I waited and waited and waited!

When I glanced their way, I could see they were in heavy conversation. I waited!

Even though I tried to keep my glances at a minimum, I couldn't help but notice after a while that Dana was becoming more and more animated. Not in a good way. I knew my daughter well, and I recognized not in a good way when I saw it. I waited!

For forty-five minutes I waited, and at last Dana jumped out, slammed the door, threw her duffle bag in the back seat of my car, slammed the door, jumped in my car, and slammed the door.

"Go!" she ordered. "Go!" She didn't look back. She didn't wave. And there was certainly no sisterly kiss blown through the breeze, the kind you would expect to see when best friends part.

The look on her face was the look you save for someone who has killed your pet parakeet. She was steaming! Smoke was coming out her nostrils.

I bit my tongue!

"The nerve of him," she said. "You'll never believe it! You will *ne-ver in a million years* believe it!"

I bit my tongue.

"Mother, I am so mad!" she said. "He loves me." It was like she'd just been proposed to by the Ayatollah! She slapped the dashboard for punctuation.

I bit my tongue.

"He's loved me for years. Can you believe it?"

I bit my tongue.

"Know what he said? He said he wants to get married but he can't wait for me forever." She slapped the dashboard.

"He says he'll have to find someone else if I won't marry him. Can you believe that?" Another slap on the dashboard.

I bit my tongue.

"'Of course, find someone!' I told him. 'Of course, get married! We're just best friends. Always were, always will be.'"

There was quiet for a moment, followed by another slap on the dashboard. I noticed that her poor hand was bright red from the trauma.

As for me, I was thinking I could taste blood running down my throat as a result of my tongue biting! I wondered if the emergency room in the next town was equipped to handle severe carpal tunnel syndrome and tongue biting trauma.

"I'll tell you one thing, though," she said, eyes flashing. The dashboard punctuation was now coming with every word she expelled. "Who*ever* he marries better understand our relationship!"

I could contain myself no longer. I burst out laughing. I'd just taken a mouthful of iced tea, and I spewed it all over me, the dashboard, and the windshield.

"What?" she screeched like a banshee, her face now between me and the road, presenting another problem that might end in the trauma center.

"I can promise you," I said, "whoever he marries *won't* understand the relationship."

It was quiet the rest of the way home.

The friendship somehow continued—unchanged as far as I could tell. In the fall, Dana told us that Barry had a girlfriend. In October she asked us if we could get a ticket for the girl for Praise Gathering. We agreed, and Dana made arrangements for us to meet up with her at our hotel. Just before we left for Indianapolis, Dana phoned.

"Call me as soon as you meet her, and tell me what she's like. Barry Shafer deserves the best. In fact, he deserves *perfect*. This girl needs to be perfect."

Somehow our plans for meeting went awry and we never laid eyes on the girl; we left her ticket at the desk. When we arrived home, Dana was on our doorstep.

"So what's she like? Is she witty, and clever? And fun? Barry's the funnest person in the world. He needs somebody fun. Does she love the Lord? Nobody loves the Lord more than Barry Shafer. Is she cute? Is she pretty? Is she right for Barry?" Wayne and I were ready!

"Oh, I don't know," I said, taking my time. "I guess you could say she's . . . (I'm milking it for all it's worth) . . . she's cuddly." Wayne shook his head in agreement.

"*Cuddly? CUDDLY?*" Dana screeched, eyes flashing. "She's *cuddly?* What kind of a person is that?"

The next event in the saga of Dana and Barry was a ski trip by the same faithful foursome, followed the very next weekend by a visit by Barry to Nashville. That surprised me, since they'd just been together, but as usual we planned a big family dinner.

After the meal as we sat around the living room, I noticed that Dana was sitting on the floor by Barry's chair. Was I mistaken, or was she leaning against his leg? Was I mistaken, or was she looking at him like he was Tom Cruise? Was I mistaken or every time he opened his mouth was she confusing him with Billy Graham?

Then the clincher! He reached out and stroked her hair! This in itself could be the eighth wonder of the world, because Dana cannot stand to have her hair touched. From the time she was a small child, her hair was off limits. I always blamed it on the fact that she had such heavy hair, it actually gave her pain to have it messed with. Whatever the reason, you just didn't go there. But Barry was going there! And she was behaving like a dopey little kitten. She was loving it! She was all but purring!

Later, we pieced together the story. She had turned around on the ski slopes to see him skiing toward her, and her heart leaped out of her body. She threw him down right there in the snow, did heavens knows what (a mother doesn't want to know!), and the rest is history.

Like I said, when it comes to your children, you should just bite your tongue and pray (knowing in your heart you have the answers). I just don't always take my own advice.

I'll Take All the Help I Can Get!

Years ago when my husband was involved in the music business, I remember a song written by Lanny Wolfe that I liked very much. I think I particularly liked it for the melody and the harmony. But it's the words that have stayed with me through the years:

> Someone is praying for you
> Remember someone is praying for you
> When you feel you're all alone,
> and your heart will break in two
> Remember, someone is praying for you.
>
> —LANNY WOLFE,
> "SOMEONE IS PRAYING FOR YOU"

The reason that song has stayed with me is that I have lived long enough now to know how important it is to have a prayer network in my life.

When I think back over my journey, I have to say that there have been so many times my own prayer life was put on the back burner because I was so weighed down with the immediate crisis: turning points like the fourteen-year ordeal of my husband's cancer and his final journey home, the death of both my parents, and the tragic loss of my sweet boy, Tom. Thankfully, I have always had a network of prayer warriors to call on. This network picks up the slack! When I have said, "I can't pray," they have said, "We will pray for you!"

Since my son's death, I have received many expressions of love, sympathy, and concern. Each of them has been such a comfort to me. The ones I cling to most share this thought, a thought my friend Carla said so well when she wrote, "We are thinking of you, and our thoughts have become prayers in your behalf."

One such letter was written by a young man who is a close friend of our family. He grew up around our kitchen table, fished off our boat dock, played on our tennis court, and took most of our family trips with us. Matt, just like my own boys, teases me unmercifully! He is like one of mine. What Matt said to me in his note will live in my heart forever. I want to share it because it is good information. But I also want to share it because it is important to be reminded never to underestimate our place in the network of prayer. We have been called to carry each other's burdens; that's what the body of Christ is all about! May Matt's words give you comfort and peace in the same way they comforted me.

Peggy,

Today in my quiet time (which is hard to find around here!) I have been thinking about you. And so I spent most of my prayer time praying for you. The scripture verses that came to mind as I prayed were 2 Corinthians 1:3–4, about how God comforts us that we may comfort others with the same comfort He gives, and Hebrews 4:16, "Let us therefore draw near with confidence to the throne of grace, that we may receive mercy and may find grace to help in time of need." How these living words of our Comforter ring true in my own life!

There was a great article in the April edition of The Lutheran *magazine by a woman who had lost three children: one at birth, one to suicide, and one to an automobile accident. The subject was "healing" from these tragedies in our lives. She made the point that when Christ arose from the grave, having defeated death and appropriating all of those wonderful gifts for His own children, He still had the scars. The wounds heal, but the scars do not go away.*

When I see a mental image of Christ's nail-pierced hands, I do not think about them being what held Him to the cross as much as I see them as a reminder that He has shared in all my sorrows. He is victorious . . . but He still has scars!

And so I pray that Peggy Benson will see her own terrible wounds heal over time and that her scars will connect her more powerfully with the Comforter.

I love you,
Matt.

May these words remind us to keep connected to the Comforter, never to underestimate the power of prayer nor the importance of it in someone's life. When God brings a friend's need to mind, remember the words of Lanny's song, and pray, pray, pray! Matt closed his letter to me with this prayer from his Lutheran Tradition:

> As you go on your way . . . May Christ go with you . . .
> May he go before you to show you the way.
> May he go behind you to encourage you,
> Beside you to befriend you,
> Above you to watch over you,
> Within you to give you peace!

"Now that I'm old enough to know better..."

I Realize I've Been Praying Wrong My Whole Life

Wayne and I began to pray for our babies before they were born. It felt rather silly at first, praying for a little blob that made my tummy stick out. Mostly we prayed that "it" would be healthy. And happy, of course! Perhaps Wayne prayed that "it" would be a boy; I've read that most men hope for a boy the first time around. But after about thirty seconds of holding Dana in his arms, he was silly in love and was ready for a house full of girls.

Soon after each of our daughters was born, we were part of a sacred service in our church committing them to God. Kind of a promise to do our part to raise them in a spiritual environment and an acknowledgement that God had our permission to do His part. The congregation was then asked to raise hands promising to support us in our efforts and to pray for us. And just as the congregants had their hands in the air, past the point of no return (and this happens somewhere in the world every Sunday in churches of every persuasion when a baby is baptized or dedicated, as the case may be), the pastor added, "and not just to pray but also to willingly work in the church nursery." Sometimes you can almost hear the screech of brakes as hands jerk to a halt. The next time you are in such a service, note the smug look on the minister's countenance after he pulls off this coup.

When our girls began to walk, we prayed that they would be safe, that they wouldn't ride their little tricycles into the street and be hit by a car, that they wouldn't fall from the top of the slide. And we prayed that they would be happy.

I beseeched God often that He not let my persistent nightmare come true, the one in which the girls and I were stalled on a railroad crossing and a train was coming toward us full speed. As I prayed that prayer, I would rehearse my dream, how I dove over the seat, grabbed them, and frantically ran to safety, where we watched the car become an inferno. Sometimes I got the car started in the nick of time, so in the nick of time that I felt the car shudder from the draft of the train missing my rear bumper by inches. Either outcome caused me to wake up in a sweat.

My mother, not knowing about my dream (I've never told a soul until now), said to me one day, "The things you anticipate in life, the things you worry about, almost never happen. The things that do happen, you couldn't have planned for." That helped! It also helped to be one of the first families in town to buy a small car—a Mustang. In my dream, I could reach the girls more easily. There was another advantage to a small car. It put them in swatting range when they sassed me or fought each other!

You know exactly what I prayed as the girls entered their teenage years! If you are a mother, you've memorized the script. Don't let her get killed in a car wreck. Don't let her hang out with the wrong crowd. Don't let her be attracted to the wrong boy. Don't let her get pregnant. Help her be interested in her schoolwork. Don't let her fail algebra. And puh-leeze, God, let her be happy.

When they were in college, and afterward, I quit giving God specific orders: "Dear God, I have no earthly idea what's going on with my daughter right now, but You do. It's in Your hands." Then, just in case I couldn't trust Him, I had to add, "Just don't let anything happen to her. And for heaven's sake, let her be happy."

I never failed to pray the happy part. And I always pointed out to the girls what would make them happy, like hanging out with the right people, going to church, eating properly, getting enough rest—the list goes on. And if you talked to either of my daughters about this, they would say that I added to the list the things that would make me happy: cleaning their rooms, helping with chores, pulling their hair out of their eyes, wearing the cutey dresses I'd bought instead of jeans. They would describe a sort of "if mama's happy, everybody's happy" lifestyle. Works for me!

Not long ago, we—Dana and her husband, Barry, Mindy, Wayne, and I—sat peacefully at the breakfast table long after the coffee had grown cold, each of us aware, I'm sure, of the years when we rarely sat peacefully together. It suddenly occurred to me that we are happy. This despite the fact that Dana, who is thirty-six, has just been diagnosed with breast cancer and the fact that Mindy is experiencing overwhelming discouragement as she tries to find her way back after years of bad decisions.

"While we are all together," I say, "I want to tell you something important." (This is hard for me to say; I can barely get the words out, but I'm compelled to say it.) "All of your lives I've prayed that you would be happy. This past year I've stopped praying that."

"Thanks a lot!" the girls responded in unison. We laughed.

"My prayer for you is that you'll know God."

It was quiet for a moment, and I thought I saw some puzzled looks. Since then, both of my precious girls have come to me to say thank you and to assure me that my prayer is being answered. Slowly but surely. And my guess would be not in the ways I could have planned or even dreamed.

Come, Lord Jesus

—Gloria

Come, Lord Jesus, at the end.
Break, then mend the waiting heart.

—MADELEINE L'ENGLE

Come; come when my lips tell You to go.
Come when I turn my back
   and walk away.
Come when I embrace the night;
   come bring the dawn of some new day.
Come with natal freshness
   when my soul is withered,
      dry with age—
When I am stuck within my story,
   come, thou hand that turns the page.
Come, thou tides of restless mercy,
   wash up on my shifting sand.
Come when I, unsteady, waver—
   be the strong and staying hand.
I—unfaithful, fickle—
   wander after glitter, charming grace—
Come, throw pretense into shadow
   by the blinding beauty of Your face.

Confessions about . . .

Life-Shaping Moments

Rembrandt, Ziploc Bags, and a Blankie

—Sue

It's not exactly surprising that my life-shaping moments have to do with old boyfriends. After all, this book *is* about confessions, isn't it? Of course, Joy's epiphanies come from literature and time spent at the seashore. As for Peggy, her watershed times can most often be found in stories of Bob, her children, and her grandchildren. And birds! Peggy can look out the window and have a life-shaping moment.

Even though we've seen Gloria in her underwear, without makeup, and with her hair uncombed, Joy, Peg, and I never cease to be amazed at the insights of this woman. "I wish I'd thought of that" and "I'd give anything to express myself as she does" are common exclamations among the three of us. She is Rembrandt, and more, when it comes to painting vivid pictures of her life-shaping moments.

Now here's something interesting! Some of our pet peeves (about inanimate objects, for heaven's sake!) have ended up in this section because they didn't fit anyplace else in the book. Go figure! For instance, when you read Gloria's piece "People Seldom Make Me Furious; It's Inanimate Objects That Drive Me Crazy," you'll be surprised out of your mind. I'm sure you never in your wildest could have imagined Gloria going a little crazy over alarm clocks, Ziploc bags, and plastic containers that won't burp. Again, it's confessions time at the ole corral!

We read each other's pieces, listen to each other's hearts, and learn. My favorite stories in this section are Peggy's, perhaps because I know the deep waters she's gone through this year. In "Moments Aren't Just 'For the Birds,'" Peggy entertains me with imaginary conversations between birds, draws me into the musings of her soul, and teaches me about the joy of living in the moment. And who but Peggy could, in her own simple way, craft a story around a security blankie?

Each of us has had hurts, big ones like the ones Peggy experienced through the loss of her loved ones, and not so big ones (at least in comparison) like I describe in "I Know When My Stomach Can't Take Another Hit." Like Joy, we've learned to walk on eggshells at times and learned perhaps the alternative is not walking at all. And we've had fears and have cried out with Gloria in groans (as she does in her poetic prayer at the close of this section) because we too have no words.

I Know the Value of My Blankie!

I am the grandmother of fourteen grandchildren ranging in age from two years to twenty-five. I have noticed through the years that they have attached themselves to one or two possessions that keep showing up even to this day, though they (the possessions, not the children) are long since past their beauty or their usefulness. Something like a favorite stuffed animal or toy or maybe a soft, once-pretty blanket that now looks soft all right but no longer pretty. In fact, to the eye of a person not aware of its importance, such a blanket may look like something that fell out of the ragbag, hardly worth noticing.

I've seen these blankies several times before, not only at my grandchildren's homes but also in their luggage when they come to spend the night at my house. I welcome these symbols of the childish need for security and comfort. It's okay with me if my grandchildren stay little and young and innocent as long as they can. The world gets to them far too quickly. Words of comfort, much less a soft touch or a hug, are soon harder to come by. So I console myself, smiling and thinking that as

77

long as they still have use for a blanket, maybe they aren't growing up too fast after all!

I've been thinking a lot these days about the significance of the blankie. I am at a place in my life where I wish I could just go and get my blanket, lie down on the couch, and have my mother come and tell me, "Everything is going to be all right. Take a nap, rest for a while, and things will get better." The comfort of a mother and a father or even a grandmother is a wonderful thing. Unfortunately, somehow life dictates to us that at some point we must give up the blankie, grow up, move forward, and learn to "keep on keeping on."

Several months ago, I was riding along in the car with my friend Barbara. I can't quite remember what all we did that morning. Probably one of our favorite activities like walking and talking, or eating and talking, or looking in plant stores and talking. Anyway, the phone in her car rang and it was Patrick, my youngest son. He was calling to tell me something that would change my life forever . . . again! My son Tom, who had gone hiking on one of his favorite mountain trails, had just been found at the bottom of a 150-foot bluff. My beautiful, sweet, blond boy was gone from me and from this earth forever.

Tom was thirty-five years old. The father of two lovely children, he was engaged to be married again after living alone for ten years. He was my friend, and because we were both single again, we leaned on each other for support. He was strong and handsome and funny, and just mischievous enough to make him interesting. He loved the Lord and all His creation. His work was in the soil, and the smell of the earth was a good smell to him. In fact, dying in the middle of the forest is the way he would have wanted to die, if he were choosing. But it was not the way I wanted it. He was supposed to take care of me and very often assured me that I need not worry because he planned to.

So just between you and me, I am at a place in my life where I don't feel like keeping on keeping on! I would like to just sit down right where I am and not think or feel anything. Because it hurts to think and feel, and the child in me says, "Find your blankie and lie down for a while."

Even as I write these words, I think of a line from an old movie theme: "What's It All About, Alfie?" I never saw the movie, so I am not sure if Alfie ever found out, but I do know that right now in my life, I don't have a clue about what is happening to me and the people I love. I don't know what it's all about! One person says to me, "Hold on; it will get better." The next one says, "Let go of the pain, and God will tell you what to do." What should I do? Hold on or let go?

In 2 Corinthians, Paul offers these words of encouragement to the church at Corinth:

> All praise to the God and Father of our Master, Jesus the Messiah! Father of all mercy! God of all healing counsel! He comes alongside us when we go through hard times, and before you know it, he brings us alongside someone else who is going through hard times so that we can be there for that person just as God was there for us.
>
> —2 CORINTHIANS 1:3–5 MESSAGE

Hold on a minute! Is Paul saying it's time for me to give up my blankie? That because I know what it is to have the comfort of the Holy Spirit in my life, I am supposed to share that comfort? In his book, *Living Prayer,* my son Robert says it this way: "The gift of our brokenness is often the only gift that we can give or receive with any real honesty and with any real hope and with any real power. We do not demonstrate our faith when we live in the light; we show our faith when we live in the dark."

And so I will keep on keeping on. I go on doing the work God has given me to do. Even when I'd rather lie down or give up! I will accept the gift of my brokenness and allow Him to use it for His glory. There are days when I feel as if I will never learn to live with this loss. But every day I am thankful for my security blanket . . . the presence of the One who knows the way, the One who touches me where the pain is unbearable, and the One who said, "I will be with you always, even until the end."

There's Just Something about Water

Edmund Wilson, renowned and widely traveled twentieth-century American author, once said, "I have had a good many more uplifting thoughts, creative and expansive visions, while soaking in comfortable baths or while drying myself after bracing showers in well-equipped American bathrooms than I have ever had in any cathedral." This strange little epigraph over a newspaper article on aromatherapy caught my attention and got me to thinking. Hey, it's true. I am much more often soothed, consoled, stimulated by a simple encounter with water than by any experience or structure, however magnificent, created by man.

The physical and emotional benefit of soaking in a warm bath up to one's chin in bubbles while breathing in the aroma of scented oils is more often a recurring dream than reality for most busy women. But Mr. Wilson's observation is one that evokes a sympathetic response in all of us. I remember when, as a mother of toddlers or teenagers, a retreat to the relaxing warmth and security of privacy, away from household din, was indeed a healing balm for body, soul, and mind. A time away from interruption. One of the few occasions when you could really let go and still be in control of your environment. No one else was going to decide the temperature or the water level. But I think the truth in this kind of experience reaches much farther than the superior equipment of the American bathroom, farther than the escape from life's pressures. It's something about the water itself that is so restorative: the soothing quality, the slight floating sensation, the mental and physical therapeutic power of its touch against the body, the sensation of its embrace, its protective, sustaining supportiveness, the refreshment of rehydration to our withered bodies and souls, its tactile cleansing and purifying.

Ancient civilizations understood water's powers. Much of what we read of the Greeks and Romans (other than when they were at war) is associated with their famous baths. Today's resorts and spas and an abundance of natural springs still attract thousands who seek relief from stress and physical affliction. But the sophistication of ornamented or controlled experiences with water are not needed to effect the desired results.

Remember running through the sprinkler and splashing in puddles as a kid? Or standing face up in a summer shower, trying to catch raindrops on your tongue? Or bobbing in ocean waves, savoring the smooth but quickening wash over your body? I like to recall both the exhilaration and refreshment of lying on the surface of a cool pool, arms dangling, moving only enough to keep afloat, looking up at the sky and feeling sandwiched between white cumulus clouds and the water's surface, strangely cozy and comforted, palpably aware of my place in the universe.

Of course, my preference is always for that greater body that is infused with salt and spreads itself irrevocably between the seven continents, splashing shore upon shore in a demonstration of unharnessed power, beauty, and grandeur. One only has to hear or see it to experience its unparalleled restorative qualities. The longer I live, the less I understand God's calling me to thirty-some years of living away from an ocean. What can He be thinking? It can't be that He doesn't get it. He Himself was sorrowful when He had to leave His beloved Galilee home and turn His face toward

Jerusalem. (I also have noticed in my reading of His story that He had little or nothing to do with creating cities.) Inland life is inhumane!

Books and articles about water therapy suggest that human beings have an affinity to water because of our beginnings in the womb, the source of our being. Perhaps that explains our fascination with water, but another consideration resonates at an even deeper level than the nourishment of a mother's womb: the life-giving Living Water Himself.

This is the water with which the Scripture is brim full. The metaphors there are many, strong, and meaningful: purification of the earth by the flood; the salvation of the children of Israel and their flocks on the wilderness journey, available just at the time they were thirsty; again, the purifying agent in the preparation of Aaron and his sons for the priesthood; and the visible cleansing agent for leprosy, a symbol of sin in Old Testament stories. Elijah's contest with the prophets of Baal, the crossing of the Red Sea out of Egypt, the changing of water to wine, the calming of the waves and walking on the waters at Galilee—all demonstrations of God's power. Perhaps the most touching of the biblical metaphors is the baptism of Jesus by water, signifying the purification of a fleshly body from sin, so that the human mind could understand that redemption from sin was necessary before Christ could present His bride, the church, to the Father in flawless perfection. That's us standing there "in full assurance of faith, having our hearts sprinkled from an evil conscience and our bodies washed with pure water" (Heb. 10:22 KJV).

That's an exhilarating thought. (Better than any warm bath or seaside cottage.) But get this! Here we are, standing in all our unglory at the throne in Revelation 22, and "the Spirit and the bride say, Come. . . . Let him that is athirst come. And whosoever will, let him take the water of [eternal] life freely" (v. 17 KJV). Wow!

Perhaps, in this world, God keeps me landlocked because He wants me to experience the intermittent refreshment of the sea rather than come to worship it. It would be easy for me to make a seaside home my idol rather than a periodic refuge for a parched body and soul. At His calling, I am invited to come to this unimaginably magnificent place and be eternally at home there, but only if I really need and want the water! I have to be thirsty.

Maybe that's why I don't live by the sea.

I Know That If Your Old Boyfriend Doesn't Remember You, It's Because He's Senile, Not Because You Didn't Make an Impact!

Before my first book, *I'm Alive and the Doctor's Dead,* came out, the publisher asked me to contact the various people I'd written about and make sure they didn't mind seeing their names in print. It was unlikely, they said, that a person would object, but we should cover our bases. In some cases they suggested I change a person's name, such as in the case of one of my doctors who blatantly lied to me.

One of the individuals I tracked down was a high school boyfriend. Such a nice boy! Sure, I could have changed his name from Ray to Elmer, but I must tell you, finding him sounded fun. Why not? There was nothing embarrassing in our past that would make talking to him awkward, unless you consider kissing and hugging a sin. I'd often wondered where he was and what he was doing, and this was my chance to find out. Of course I hoped he'd had a happy, healthy life. Of course I wished for him a buttercup of a wife and little dimpled, brown-eyed children. I'm not sure how dimples shake down, but everyone knows the brown-eye gene is predominant! And oh, Ray's eyes! Never mind . . . I'm rambling . . . let's move on.

I'll admit I desperately wanted to hear Ray's strong, youthful voice pulse with recognition. Face it! I wanted to think he'd been waiting by the phone hoping I'd call. Okay, so I thought he might still be carrying just a tiny little itsy-bitsy torch for me, that on rare occasions, like when he got in a fight with his wife, he wondered what it would have been like had the two of us ridden off into the sunset in that pink and black Ford convertible of his.

Remembering Ray had lived in the very small town of Milton, West Virginia, I called directory assistance. "Lots of Harbours," the operator told me, "but no Rays." Next I called the high school, and when I mentioned that I was an author, it was VIPs'ville! I was put straight through to the principal.

"I'm trying to track down a former student," I said, "from the fifties, so you may not remember. Ray Harbour is the—"

"Sure, I know Ray. Nice boy! I know all the Harbours. Town's full of 'em," he said. "So you're an author . . . how 'bout that."

I assured him this wasn't some murder investigation or expose but simply a life story kind of thing and that Ray was barely mentioned.

"Well, I can tell you this," he said eagerly. Ray married that girl, Peggy; her family owns the flower shop. They moved away from here, you know. Years ago. Florida. Right! They moved to Florida. Ray senior died a while back. Maybe five years ago."

I didn't know Ray's dad, but I made a note.

"I'm thinkin', I'm thinkin'." I could practically hear the rubber burning. "Here's what you do; you call Tommy. He's the mayor—matter'fact he's a Harbour himself; he knows everything and everybody." He gave me the number. "So you're writin' a book? How 'bout that?"

The mayor's wife answered the phone. "So you're writin' a book? How 'bout that." She sounded flustered. "My goodness, my goodness!" she exclaimed. I made my speech.

"I cannot believe this," she said. "Tommy will have a fit he missed you. He knows all the Harbours, but I can tell you this: nice boy that Ray! Ray married Peggy over at the flower shop, and I know for sure they moved away years ago. Florida, I think. Ray senior died; did you know that?"

"Yes, I heard," I said. "Must of been four or five years ago now."

"A book! How 'bout that. Well, tell you what, call the flower shop. I'm lookin', I'm lookin'," she said, and I could hear the pages rustling. "Here's the number. But promise me whether you get hold of Ray or not you'll call back and talk to Tommy. He'll just love you to pieces."

Next I dialed the flower shop and explained my situation. "Oh my goodness, Ray and Peggy, Ray and Peggy, Ray and Peggy! I'm going through a drawer right now as I talk to you, looking for their number. Ray was a nice boy! You say you write books? Well, I'll be! I'm lookin', I'm lookin'. Peggy's a cousin, I should know it by heart. You know they moved away, don't you? Florida. I'm lookin'. Ray senior died; did you know that?"

"I did!" I exclaimed.

After all I'd been through and the excitement that was building, I was shaking when I dialed the number. I could picture the handsome, lithe young Ray running eagerly for the phone. I was as breathless as a twitterpated teenager as I reintroduced myself and stated the purpose of my call.

"Sue? Sue *who?*" You would have thought by his tone of voice that I was selling cemetery plots. Besides that, he sounded like an old man.

"Oh, I remember," he said. "Hadn't thought of you in years. Went to Stonewall, didn't you? Lived on Mathews? Had a stupid cat, didn't you?" That reminded me of my suspicion that Ray had killed my precious darling when he spun out of the driveway our last evening together. We found our precious darling dead the next morning.

"You're writin' a book, you say?" He not only sounded like an old man, he was rambling like an old man. "I never would have pictured you writin' a book. Sure, go ahead, say anything you want to."

Remember Ray? Married Peggy Sue? Her people own the flower shop downtown? Ray and Peggy moved to Florida years ago and had little brown-eyed children. Ray senior died. Oh, maybe five years ago or so. You know, it's such a shame, but I've heard Ray is well on his way to senility. His memory is practically gone. Such a shame! Nice boy that Ray, unless you call running over a cat murder!

I Realize People Seldom Make Me Furious; It's Inanimate Objects That Drive Me Crazy

Madeleine L'Engle is right. There *is* a "conspiracy of inanimate objects!" Maybe it's while we are sleeping that they get together and plot their attack. Or maybe they wink at each other while we are intent on making our well-ordered lists of what we must accomplish before the sun sets.

gloria

But I am convinced there is some malignant plan on the part of plastic containers, table legs, ketchup bottles, and other such unavoidable plagues in my life to obstruct any just and admirable goal for the day.

It starts before I even get out of bed. The alarm rings (or gurgles or chirps or rushes like the ocean tides) and I reach through the predawn darkness to turn it off before my husband hears it too, and is awakened an hour and fifteen precious minutes before he has to get up. Is there an easily felt little metal lever like the good-ole-fashioned clocks

87

used to have? Of course not! There is a sliding piece of bumpy plastic, recessed attractively into the design of the decor-driven time-telling device that is next to impossible to identify in the dark. In my frantic effort to get my finger in the indentation, I knock the stupid thing off the nightstand and it crashes, still making its "environmentally correct" sound, to the floor. I hear Bill's soft, even snore turn to a snort or two that lets me know my seconds are numbered. My impulse is to jump out of bed and seize the clock by the throat, but before I can spring into action, I find the sheet has a stranglehold on my big toe! I crash into the wall and slide down the rough plaster, getting a wall burn on one arm while I fish around with the other hand for the clock. See what I mean?

The one good thing about all this is that I am now fully awake and ready to tackle the day. I rush into the bathroom in the dark and sit on the toilet. Now I'm more than awake! The cold porcelain rim that greets my bed-warm fanny lets me know that Bill has left the seat up on his last visit in the night.

From then on I can chart my day by the assaults on my plan of action (and my intelligence) by such inanimate objects, most of which wormed their way into my life by passing themselves off as laborsaving devices.

I try to take my vitamins, for instance, and have to call my six-year-old grandson, Lee, who has spent the night, to come take off the childproof lid before I smash both the obstinate cap and the little brown bottle it's on with a sledgehammer.

I turn on the faucet for cold water to make coffee. The faucet is one of those "convenient all in one" things—you know, the kind with the sprayer inserted in the end of the faucet so you can just pull it out to spray the garbage off the plates. The problem with this is that if the last person to use it has left the sprayer facing sideways or pointed at the ceiling and I turn it on with my head turned toward the coffeepot because with the other hand I'm trying to push the filter basket into its cradle ... you guessed it! I spend the next fifteen minutes mopping water from the kitchen window, the plant shelf, and the microwave.

Then there's the safety lock on my utility vehicle. I can't count the number of times I have gotten out, my arms loaded with purse, books, and a bag or two, to go around and open the hatch or to get my granddaughter Madeleine out of her car seat only to remember that even if the doors were all unlocked when I got in, they all locked when I started the car, and only the driver's door remains unlocked. Madeleine usually screams in frustration as I walk all the way around to the only unlocked door to hit the unlock button.

This list goes on: the freshness seals on the plastic containers that don't "burp" like the lady showed you at the party, where you bought three hundred dollars' worth of these colorful little bowls and squares that will "save you so much money." No, instead of burping, the lid pops off on the opposite side or the whole slick thing scoots out of your grasp, and pickled beets dump all over the new white tile, staining the grouting pink for the rest of your days. And how about

- the Ziploc bags that won't zip
- squirt bottles that won't squirt (because there's an unpeelable "peel off" seal under the squirt lid)
- pump bottles of window cleaner that won't pump
- perforated "easy open" boxes of pancake flour, cereal, and cake mix that take a kitchen knife to break the perforation
- ballpoint pens that won't write but will leak great purple globs of congealed ink through the leather of your new white purse

Machinery fills the ranks of another whole army of evil conspirators. Who hasn't had her day demolished by the water softener that won't soften, the sump pump that won't sump, and the dishwasher that needs you to wash the dishes before you load it so the forks won't have dried spinach leaves clinging to the tines?

Who hasn't had to do push-ups at night to keep up the muscle tone she's going to need to wrestle the sheets and bra straps from the tentacles of the washing machine agitator? What self-respecting woman hasn't taken the scissors to the front of a marvelous silk blouse before she would admit she'd been outsmarted by the contrary back-loaded zipper? Who hasn't switched to a not-so-cool leather watchband so she didn't have to admit she just couldn't add to her life trying to cope with those fold-in, fold-out watchbands that, if you cross them, pinch a piece out of your tender wrist?

Technology forms a battalion so formidable I'm not sure I even want to take it on. No, I do not have a computer! I'm writing this on a yellow legal pad with my handheld pencil. Let some braver, more stouthearted soul transfer it to "disk." I also hate things without a soul that talk back to me. "Fasten your seat belt." "Your tank is empty." "The number you have entered is invalid." "The disk is full; cannot accept information."

Shoot! If somebody isn't going to accept input, I'd rather it be my husband. I can work on him over time. I can change my attitude. I can bake an apple pie and promise to come to bed earlier. Or I can just chalk it up to the stubborn streak in him.

But deliver me from pigheaded inanimate objects. Give me an opponent with a brain any day. Any woman I know can outthink, outmaneuver, or outtalk any thinking adversary. But when it comes to the frontal attacks by inanimate objects, I surrender! Give me the good ole days before technology and laborsaving devices!

Sacred Memories

In my experience teaching high school seniors advanced placement English, I have become enamored with the life lessons of Fyodor Dostoevsky—both those he learned in the context of his own horrendous struggles and those that grab at my heart from the pages of his timeless fiction. The last couple of years, *The Brothers Karamazov* has been the senior summer reading assignment. Seven-hundred-plus translated pages whose words I have found the most exhilarating, the most enlightening, and without question the most personally reproving I have experienced in classic literature. I am consummately condemned by the totality of personal characteristics I see in the Karamazov family, for indeed they are all me, and what I am brought both to love and hate in them, I cherish and despise in myself. But as edified as I am by their story, I am even more delighted—and surprised—at another lesson garnered from their creator: "You are told a lot about your education, but some beautiful, sacred memory, preserved since childhood, is perhaps the best education of all. If a man carries many such memories into life with him, he is saved for the rest of his days. And even if only one good memory is left in our hearts, it may also be the instrument of our salvation one day."

My first reaction to that assertion was one of perplexity: childhood memories are lovely, but how might they be so significant in a distant future redemption? I began sifting through the treasures of my childhood, at first reminiscing merely for pleasure. My thoughts took me back to halcyon summer days I spent at the sprawling country home of my grandparents during my elementary school years. I remembered Sunday afternoons when, more often than not, the "Gowanda relatives" arrived, and my grandmother allowed me to assist her in serving tall, cool glasses of lemonade and sugar cookies, which of course necessitated the donning of a stiff-starched, white, embroidered apron and walking ever so cautiously, balancing a silver tray. For me, it was the perfect assimilation of the Jane Austen novels and *Little Women*.

On weekdays, I was at my leisure to sit in the huge backyard maple with perfectly crotched places from which to master the helm of a huge ship, feeling every sinew of the power in John Masefield's "Sea Fever."

> I must go down to the seas again,
> Down to the seas and the sky.
> And all I ask is a tall ship
> and a star to steer her by.

Nothing but a smooth sail and a safe landing ever crossed my imagination.

I swung in the long-roped board swing that hung from that tree, pumping with all of my six- or seven-year-old might until I was nearly parallel with the earth, singing at the top of my voice Robert Louis Stevenson's "The Swing."

Oh how I love to go up in a swing,
Up in the air so blue.
Oh I do think it's the pleasantest thing
Ever a child can do.
Up in the air and over the wall
Til I can see so wide
Rivers and trees and cattle and all
Over the country side.

I'll never forget roaming through Grandpa's wheat fields in grains taller than myself and mushing down the stalks (a no-no) to make little nests or rooms, from the floor of which I lay watching birds and cloud formations move overhead, listening to the winds play across the heads of grain, thinking aloud the lines from Stevenson's "The Wind."

I saw you toss the kites on high
And blow the birds about the sky
And all around I heard you pass
Like ladies' skirts across the grass . . .

Guess what! All these years later, those lines of poetry and hundreds more that were part of my childhood repertoire come flashing back to lift me and delight me, often at moments when I am in sore need of comfort and restoration. They are now the invisible unstressor of my day, a bit of substance that places me in the universe, both physically and between past and future—a very present link between the comfort of those relationships, now gone for the moment but promising to reappear when we are reunited in heaven. Who would have thought that nursery rhymes my mother sing-songed to me from cradle days, great books to which she introduced me, and years of carefree play, the gift of loving grandparents, would bring me such joy over sixty years later? God. Dostoevsky. Yes.

Not all of my happy childhood memories are associated with literature. However, now and then, I find myself trying to share the enchantment of those childhood treasures with my senior high students. Though they don't quite get it, I quote on with abandonment while they either smile in amused contentment or stare in awe—not enraptured by the poetry but stunned by the thought that this is a picture of what they could become should they allow themselves to be caught up in the reveries of an old lady and her poetry.

Back to Dostoevsky. I don't think it was the charm or contentment or even the comfort of the time and place and verse revisited that would be significant to his lesson. But perhaps if a man (or in this case, a woman) has such a childhood memory to savor, then just maybe it is easier for her to understand the beauty of the resurrection story—the story which so powerfully penetrates the human heart that it gives birth to salvation!

Listen to the Sea

—Gloria

I praise You, O God,
For giving every creature what it needs.
The gulls float on the ocean teeming with
    fish.
They walk the sandy beach where Your
    waves have carried
        and buried scallops and clams.
The fish swim where the minnow and tiny
    shrimp hatch in oversufficient numbers.
The whales find what they need in each gulp
    of seawater ... and it's already salted!
For the plant eaters, there is kelp.
The dove picking along the ground finds
    the seeds of the grasses,
        while the pelican scoops along
            with his sharp eyes
        that spot a silvery movement in the
    water a hundred feet away.
Am I, too, sitting right on top of what I
    need?
Has the marvel of Your provision placed me
    in the richest feeding ground
        for my particular hungers?

Forgive me for expecting more miracles
    when I *am* a miracle,
        living in a bed of miracles.
Today You will feed me where I am.

I Know That Not All Sacraments Are Given in Church

The hot sun bore down on the holiday beach-bathers lined up on their oversized designer towels. The smell of seaweed and ocean tides mingled with the sweet aroma of coconut oil and piña colada tanning lotion. The breeze was welcome, but not quite enough to cool the bottoms of feet baked by walks in the hot sand.

I was one of these overtired, over-scheduled escapees to the island. I was lying on my stomach reading a book when I felt a gentle sensation trickling over my feet.

"There," said Jesse. "I'm getting all the sand off, Mamaw. I'm washing your feet."

A quick glance over my shoulder and I saw my five-year-old grandson dipping water from a little green pail with his sand shovel, then pouring each measured portion over my sandy, burning feet.

"All clean, Mamaw. Now doesn't that feel better?"

97

The cool baptism was more than sacred to me. It had been only forty-eight hours since Jesse had been rushed by helicopter to Boston Children's Hospital. Suzanne had been the only one allowed to travel the thirty-minute trip with Jesse, her sweet boy confined in a neck brace and taped to a body board. I had followed by plane with Jesse's daddy, Barry.

It had happened so fast. Suzanne and seven-year-old Will had gone on to the hotel from the beach on their bikes; Jesse and Barry were to follow, giving Jesse a bit more time to play in the waves. Riding home, Jesse got hot and thirsty and asked to stop for a drink. After waiting for a safe place to leave the bike trail to cross the busy road, they started across to the small store.

"Come on, Jesse," said Barry, "let's go."

But for some reason Jesse was distracted and didn't follow right away. By the time he had started across, a car appeared around a curve, going too fast for the busy holiday weekend.

Barry watched in horror as the car struck his child. Seeming to move in slow motion, as in a bad movie, Jesse's little body was thrown into the windshield, then was hurled about twelve feet beyond the car to land face down on the pavement.

"It's Jesse," Barry's shaken voice said when Bill answered the phone.

"What is it, Barry? What's happened?"

"I think he'll be all right. Come to the hospital. Bring Suzanne. I couldn't get her on the phone."

Now *we* were moving like a bad slow-motion movie. Down the stairs, into the car, into the cottage to get Suzanne and Will, through the tiny vacation-crowded streets, through the hospital corridors.

"It's routine. We have no pediatric unit here. We always life-line children to Boston."

But the reassuring tone in the nurse's voice wasn't nearly reassuring enough. We awaited every X ray, every blood test, every CAT scan with an anxiety we weren't able to put to rest.

I stood with Will and Barry and Bill watching helplessly as my daughter and her little son lifted off in the helicopter. She waved weakly from the window—a wave reminiscent of the one she gave as a child through the window of the tiny commuter the first time we all said good-bye to this island.

Over the years, our family had kept up a love affair with this magical place, and now we had returned with a new generation to make memories.

But this was not the sort of memory we had hoped to make.

"Please, God. You go with them. Go with us all," I breathed.

In a short time that seemed like an eternity, Barry and I waited with Suzanne for more test results.

"Because of the mechanics of the accident, we need a few more pictures." We listened to that sentence over and over. With the return of each piece of film, each scan, each test, the doctors would shake their heads.

"You are a fortunate little boy," they would say to Jesse. "Tell all your friends to always wear their bike helmets like you did."

The doctors had wanted to keep him overnight, so we kept a vigil. He amazingly slept like a very exhausted child would and awakened wanting something to eat.

By noon the next day we had landed back on the island and were walking across the tarmac to meet Will and his Papaw Bill, overwhelmed by the miracle of legs that move, eyes that blink, a giggle that escapes from a mischievous little grin, and a wide little hand holding tightly to ours. The next day we were lying on the beach again, and a little boy was baptizing my feet.

Do this in remembrance of me kept going through my mind.

Jesse hadn't quite come to understand those words yet. But I understood what Simon Peter must have felt when the pure heart of God knelt to wash his feet.

"All clean," said Jesse. "You're all clean now."

And by some miracle, I was.

"Be Anxious for Nothing"

"Be anxious for nothing." Paul's exhortation to the Philippians has always puzzled me. As a teenager, my life was fairly well-ordered, secure, and carefree. I didn't have a lot of worries. Even in the immediacy of what a teenager sees as crisis, I was fairly confident that everything would turn out okay. It always had. Like most young preachers' families of that decade, we "couldn't afford" many of life's luxuries, but we had more than we needed. We got sick, but we always got better. We got our hearts broken and our egos trampled on every now and then, and parsonage life often brought us to a position of playing frontline defense for Dad, but eventually, an invisible quarterback would make a propitious call and things would smooth out. So I remember feeling encouraged as I read those words in Philippians, believing that it was a spiritual law to which I could always measure up—with only one exception.

From the time I was old enough to understand about jobs, salaries, bank accounts, and real estate, I recognized that Dad was our security. For most of those first two decades of my life, we lived in a parsonage owned by a church. Without Dad, we had no house, no meal ticket. So I grew to adulthood with the troubling fear that my father might not live until the four of us children were able to take care of ourselves, and though he was seldom sick and I knew of no impending health problem, I prayed every night that Dad would live until we were all grown.

In the fall of my twenty-second year, filled with the anticipation of a newly promised bride-to-be and the fresh-out-of-college optimism of a first-year elementary school teacher, that underlying anxiety burst suddenly into full-fledged reality, and I was flung into a state of uncertainty that still often nags at my spiritual understanding. My father died suddenly of a heart attack while driving to the home of a parishioner for whom he was to make funeral arrangements. Ironic and devastating. I couldn't imagine coming home to his absence, and I was even less ready to accept that he would not be a part of my wedding.

I am newly amazed every time I recall those first dreaded days without him. They weren't easy, but they were not at all as I had anticipated. For the God to whom Dad had introduced us as very young children was not merely faithful. He had already put into motion a powerful salving process—soothing and shrinking to band-aid size a hurt that promised to be of enormous unbearability.

Mom had returned to her teaching career a year earlier. We weren't "all grown up" as I had hoped, but now, growing quickly, we were marvelously sustained by that amazing grace that at such moments infuses lives with strength way beyond their natural emotional and spiritual maturity. We not only survived but were able to rejoice, not at losing Daddy but at his presence with the Lord and at the unexpected peace that enveloped our days without him.

However, I never really "got off the hook" on the anxiety issue. I have found a host of new things to worry about. So I'm still hanging, and I have to admit that most days, even now, I am relatively clueless as to how to respond to life's greater calamities. I waver between what seems to me to be presumptuous and what I fear may be downright disobedient. At best, I remain puzzled, ambivalent. But of this one thing I have become absolutely, unassailably confident: God can be trusted.

After all, Daddy has been gone thirty-nine years and Mom nearly twenty-five, and here are these grown-up children—a striking, fourfold example of God's mercy—alive, loved, and experiencing a sense of God's wholeness and abiding peace. My puzzlement over Philippians 4 notwithstanding, I love the way Eugene Peterson ends his paraphrase of that passage:

> Before you know it, a sense of God's wholeness, everything coming together for good, will come and settle you down. It's wonderful what happens when Christ displaces worry at the center of your life.

—VERSE 6 MESSAGE

So what's to worry? Will I ever learn?

We've Been Driving through the Mountains, Lord

—Gloria

We've been driving through the mountains,
  Lord—
    winding our way in an air-conditioned car
      up the narrow road
    cutting through the towering oaks and
      maples, pines and tulip trees.
The mountain laurel and sassafras sprouts
  are at eye level as we drive along,
    and I know the fragrance is heavenly,
      mixed with the musky smells of mosses
        and rich earth.
Why was I so timid, then, Lord, when I
  suggested we roll down all the windows?
Why was I so easily silenced when someone
  said the wind would mess up our hair?
Now, I know we will return to the flat
  plains with our hair intact,
    but not our spirits.
The mountain trails were beautiful to behold,
  but You gave us at least five senses

as avenues to transport food to our souls,
and we settled for using only sight.
We could have filled our nostrils with
fresh mountain air
fragrant with a hundred rare perfumes.
We could have heard the leathery rhythm band
of colliding oak leaves accompanying
the song of a thousand birds.
We could have felt the wind in our hair,
caressing our faces.
We could have stopped and touched the
shagbark hickories and the smooth
beeches.
We could have pulled up a small sassafras
seedling
and nibbled on a sliver of root.
We could have peeked under a tulip leaf
to find the lovely yellow and orange
blossom so rare to huge trees.
We might have stopped at one of the pull-off
places and leaned over a cliff to see
the valley below
and beheld vistas that would have
taken our breath away.
But at least, Lord, we didn't sweat and our
hair didn't get messed up.

I Know When My Stomach Can't Take Another Hit

I am the lowest I've ever been," I sobbed. "My soul is anguished. I'm at the end of the rope." This was in response to my loved one's question, "So how are you doing?" It's rare that I expose my feelings to this degree, but she knew the traumatic situation I'd been going through, and let's face it, I was desperate for understanding, comfort, and most of all hope that things would be better.

She smiled ever so sweetly. "But I thought you were so happy," she said. "You have your books and all."

Did I hear a condescending tone of voice? And *happy?* We're not exactly talking happy here. I tried to explain, but my words fell on deaf ears. She said, "Why don't you go home and analyze why you are so unhappy." I felt as though I'd been hit in the stomach by a sledgehammer. "Personally, I turn to Scripture when I'm . . ." I tried to shut my ears! Another jab to the stomach; I wanted to disappear.

Now that I'm old enough to know better, I know there will always be those with easy answers—not out of cruelty but, perhaps, out of naivete or lack of understanding. After all, understanding is often gained through life experience, and perhaps, as was true of me, the meaning of happy just hadn't soaked in. And now that I'm old enough to know better, I know there is a place I can turn to for understanding, comfort, and hope. It's the arms of the Savior, and unlike any other place, it's oh so trustworthy.

I Know That the Journey Home Means Reclaiming the Steps along the Way

gloria

It was nearly dawn. The night had been long, filled with regret and despair. Images paraded across Peter's memory, images so outrageous they seemed almost surreal: the Passover supper that broke all tradition when Jesus drank and then offered the forbidden Elijah's cup, thus proclaiming the wine and bread to be His own blood and flesh; the awkward silence after the strange interchange between Jesus and Judas; the surge of protective passion Peter had felt that made him blurt out his pledge to do anything, to go anywhere to follow his Lord; Jesus' sad prediction of Peter's denials before the cock crowed. There had been the silent walk in the darkness down the stairs from the upper room and out across the Kidron Valley to Gethsemane, and the heavy weariness that seemed to descend on them all like a fog. How could he forget Jesus' obvious disappointment that they couldn't be supportive when He seemed to need it most?

As he sorted through it all, Peter couldn't make sense of his emotions. What made him fly into such a rage and slice the ear off the soldier who stepped forward to grab Jesus by the arm? Rage and depression often walked hand in hand for Peter, and hardly had the chaos of the arrest in the garden occurred before Peter's solitude in the all-too-silent night ushered in the familiar "dark cloud."

Conflicts tore at his soul. His mind became a battlefield of self-accusation. Fierce loyalty and desperate fear arm-wrestled his resolve. Self-accusation nipped at his spirit like a pack of jackals emerging from the night.

Being alone was more than he could bear, so the gnawing sense of failure directed his stumbling steps toward the courtyard of Caiaphas's hall, where Jesus had been taken. There the smell of a charcoal fire promised some warmth for the chill in his bones. Pulling his hood forward enough to hide most of his face, he eased in to blend with the motley crew that had gathered, and he extended his hands toward the flames.

A young servant girl turned to look at the bulky figure beside her just as a breeze fanned the flames and a flash of light fell across Peter's face. "I know you! You hang around with the guy they just arrested. You're one of them!"

Before he could run the words through his mind, they were out of his mouth. "You're crazy! I never knew him!" Two others who stood around the fire rushed to confirm the girl's suspicion. And to each came the quick denial.

A sound he had ignored a hundred times before immediately broke through to his consciousness: a rooster greeting the dawn on the other side of the courtyard stable.

The crucifixion nightmare had soon followed—and the deepest plunge into depression Peter had ever known. Had not the first day of the next week dawned with such a radiant sunrise followed by the blazing light of the resurrection's good news, the attraction of suicide would have been for the first time in his life too strong to resist.

It was a good thing Jesus had said to Mary that morning, "Go tell my disciples *and Peter*." That single sentence became the lifeline with which Jesus had drawn Peter back from the pits into His intimate circle of friends. Then how like the Lord to finish the healing process for Peter through that unforgettable morning by the lake!

It was dawn again. ("Dawn" was still sensitive for Peter.) The morning mist mingled with the smoke from a charcoal fire, a fire that invited friends to gather round. Déjà vu was about to overwhelm Peter when Jesus offered him the restoring breakfast of baked fresh fish and simple barley bread. Then, knowing how his failure haunted Peter, Jesus directed his gentle question to him. "Do you *love* me?"

It was as if Jesus had offered to walk with Peter back through all the sore and sensitive places of his past. "Oh, yes!" was his quick response. "You know that I love you."

"Feed my sheep." Trust restored. Responsibility assigned. How Peter welcomed a chance to do something to make it all up to his friend.

"*Do* you love me?" Jesus' question came again.

"I *do;* you know I do."

"Feed my lambs."

Lambs, thought Peter, *the young and trusting ones. I'm being trusted with the young and trusting ones!*

This time Jesus stopped his occupation with cooking and serving to look into Peter's eyes. There was no mistaking this time; this trio of questions had definitely been for Peter.

"Do you love *me?*" said Jesus. "More than these?"

These. The pronoun hung in the air like a banner over any object Peter's life could ever fill in. "I do, Lord. It is *you* I love the most."

"Feed my sheep."

No cock crowed. The soft lapping of the water against the shoreline pebbles flowed like a gentle balm to all the cracked and fractured places in Peter's psyche. *Healed* took on a new meaning for him that day. Beyond the raising up of his mother-in-law from her sickbed. Beyond the simple "take up your bed and walk" he'd heard Jesus say the day the lame man was made well. Healed on the inside. Restoration was the marvel of this morning. Jesus had walked with Peter through every awful place to save him from the agony of guilt. Paradise regained.

Peter's experience is a model of restoration for us all. Psychiatrists who want to help people to be truly well must learn this principle: "If we confess our sins, he is faithful and just to forgive us our sins, and to cleanse us from all unrighteousness" (1 John 1:9 KJV).

"Reclaiming the places" brings healing at the deepest level. Jesus knew that Satan would use every predawn hour, every charcoal fire, every rooster crow, and every threat of depression to dredge up the past and keep Peter in bondage.

Replacing those phantom images of failure with new pure, good, restorative experiences based on honesty empowered Peter to move on in confidence and to take responsibilities without bondage.

I remember once my mother revealing an experience she had of being infatuated with a leading minister in our church movement. My parents were pastors, too, and many times Mother was in situations in which she worked with this man on state boards or national committees. He was a handsome man with admirable traits; she felt drawn to him at first by his spiritual qualities but, over time, began to realize she was attracted to him on a more human level.

She prayed about this, then tried to resist the feelings by willpower, but this course of action was ineffective. Finally, she realized what she had to do. She went to my father and said, "Lee, I want to confess something to you, and I want you to pray for me." She told her husband exactly how she had felt and confessed the mind games she had failed to conquer.

Later she told me, "Lee took me in his arms and together we got down on our knees. He prayed that this infatuation would be taken away and a sweet friendship restored. That attraction dissipated like a fog on a sunny day and never bothered me again."

How human it is for us to want to cover and deny. How divine and healing it is for us to face, confess, and then reclaim every place soiled by failure by telling the whole truth to others, to God, and to ourselves.

In my own experience it has been the places I consented to revisit with my Master that have found healing and reclamation. No longer in bondage to the sites of failure, I have been able to walk anywhere in freedom and joy. The threat of old memories fades away and becomes impotent. Every inch of territory is miraculously turned once again into holy ground.

I wonder if Peter, after he had his redeeming conversation with Jesus that morning over breakfast, suddenly recalled the rest of what Jesus had said that night He predicted Peter would fail him.

"You'll deny me three times," Jesus had said. "Don't let this throw you. You trust God, don't you? Trust me. There is plenty of room for you in my Father's home. . . . I'll come back and get you so you can live where I live" (John 13:38–14:3 MESSAGE).

This sweet promise is for us, too. "Don't let failure throw you." Words of grace. Words of hope. "I will not leave you orphaned." We will not be stranded somewhere on the other side of failure. Not only is there a way back but there is a way to get back all the places and sounds and smells and sights that could ever remind us of our failure. Face them in truth. Meet Jesus there—at the charcoal fire, in the courtyard, at the crack of dawn, in the morning mist . . . wherever the scent of failure mars a memory. We can let Jesus take us there to wrench back from the clutch of Satan all that should be good and beautiful.

> I repent for moments I have spent
> Recalling all the pain and failures of my past—
> I repent for dwelling on the thing beyond my power to
>   change—
> The chains that held me fast.
> I give up the bitterness and hate,
> And blaming men and fate for all my discontent.
> The guilt and pain I empty from my cup,
> So God can fill it up with peace and sweet content.
> I accept the promise of the dawn,
> A place to build upon to make a brand new day.
> I will begin, convinced that Jesus lives,

Assured that He forgives and that He's here to stay.
I will go on!
My past I leave behind me.
I gladly take His mercy and His love.
He is joy and He is peace;
He is strength and sweet release.
I know He is and I am His.
I will go on.

—WILLIAM J. GAITHER AND GLORIA GAITHER,
FROM "I WILL GO ON"

Moments Aren't Just "For the Birds"

It's dark and cloudy out my kitchen window this bleak January morning. It rained again last night, and so down the street that dead ends in front of my door, a small stream of water winds along a path, to be lost forever to the sewer system. All up and down the street on each side of the little stream is a small flock of birds. Mostly sparrows and maybe a few hardworking mother robins. They are drinking as fast as they can because they realize the water will soon dry up. Smart little creatures, they have learned by experience to drink up while it is plentiful.

peggy

I open the door to watch them and listen to them talk. Their chatter reminds me of the chatter I hear standing in line at the cafeteria. Maybe they are talking about the long, dry season we have had here or about how they're having trouble finding enough food with so many birds scrambling for room at the bird feeder. Maybe the conversation goes something like this:

"I don't think the worms are as plentiful as they were last spring."

"The straw and twigs for our nests are not quite as easy to come by as last year."

"Aren't the long, gray days of winter depressing?"

I have a feeling that when the rain dries up and the sun comes out, there will be other work to do and other plans to make and other drinks of water, some provided by the birdbaths of gardeners along the flight path. There won't be any time to chatter about the weather, for it will be a busy time. In the meantime, here and now is the gift of a little stream of water to quench their thirst.

These little creatures are rather plain and ordinary. They are not the flashy, showy, bright cardinals or the vivid bluebirds, and certainly not the sweet hummingbirds of summer. Perhaps colorful birds go south for winter. They seem to have more winter vacation money. Or maybe they are like me; they have more friends with winter vacation connections! It seems to me that these flash-in-the pan birds are nowhere to be seen on the dark, dreary days of January. That leaves the plain birds (mostly the mothers) to take care of home and family, to hunt for food, to replenish and refurbish, and to make plans for the spring to come. I try to do my part to help. I keep the water bowl spilling over and the bird feeder full—if only the squirrels would stay out of the birdseed.

I wonder, do these little creatures find themselves, as I do, rethinking and recalling memories of the past and wondering about the moments to come and the work that is left to be done as spring approaches? Winter seems to be a time for all of us creatures, large and small, young and old, feathers or not, to remember life as it used to be. To recall the days gone by that will never come again, and then to turn to the task of preparing for today's and tomorrow's moments.

Contemplating today and its moment and trying to look to the future, as the birds are doing, I have to ask myself some questions. Would I know a moment if it flew up and hit me in the face? Have I become so burdened with the pain of the past that I am no longer living the now of life?

This particular January morning comes only months after I buried my son. As I stand by the window watching the birds, one of these memorable moments creeps into my mind.

My husband, Bob, was speaking at a retreat. He told his audience, "Please take a sheet of paper and draw a horizontal line through the center. Above the line, write good things God has sent into your life. Then list and reflect on those moments that brought joy to your life. Below the line, write bad things and list and reflect on all the hard places that have brought you to your knees and challenged your faith." Then Bob watched as they struggled with what to write where on their lists. After he'd given them some time to work, he told them that the entire paper could be committed to God. "Remember," he said, "He is the God of the top list and the God of the list at the bottom!"

I heard him say that dozens of times to dozens of audiences. He would say to them, "In the course of your life it is interesting to note that things you have put on the bad-moments list often jump to the good list, because in the living of life you realize how much His presence has meant to you and that with His help you actually learned more about Him and about yourself." But I admit that today I am having trouble with my list. It's easy to remember the good moments of my life. I know I wouldn't be able to write fast enough to keep up with the flow. The bad-moments list is another thing. Though ideas for the list of good things flow freely, I'll start with the list of bad things. It's always been my philosophy to start by painting the darkest picture first in order to enjoy the sunshine later, when it comes. During those years when Bob was so ill, I'd say to the doctor at each visit, "Tell me the worst news first." I wanted to choke down the bad news and leave with any tidbits that might be hopeful.

So here I go in my own zany way, starting with the bottom of the page with the bad things. These are some of the things that I painfully write:

Any memory that includes the times of suffering and the death of Bob—my husband, my confidant, my best friend.

The retirement years we missed having together—long walks, little trips to see the fall leaves, watching the beach at sunset while holding each other.

I will always miss just loving him and touching him and fighting with him and then making up (which was actually a lot of fun!).

The way he made me feel so special and wanted, both in public and in private.

The way he brought joy and humor to the everydayness of our lives.

Knowing that every day with him was fun and special, even when what was happening to us wasn't fun or special!

The dignity, respect, and concern he showed me. I deeply appreciate the way he taught our children to have that same quality.

Most of all, I miss his emotional strength to help me with other hard places on my journey, like the loss of both my parents.

And finally, having to survive the death of our son Tom without his support. To this day, I can hardly believe I won't see either of them on this earth again. It is incredibly painful to write about the death of a child. Tom and death in the same sentence seems like a contradiction in terms. His was an unfinished life, gone in an instant. Though it heals over some from time to time, the hole in my heart will never go away. Basically I will always walk with a limp to remind myself how much he meant to me and to pray for other mothers who live this same nightmare.

It is indeed easier to move to the top of the list and joyfully write about the good things:

The love of a good man who loved me unconditionally.

Children who love each other and love the Lord.

A church family that has shown me the ways of the Lord.

Wonderful friends who have prayed, pushed, and prodded me along.

The gift of health. The strength and opportunity to pursue new work and new ways to serve. Places to speak and books to write.

Oh yes, I mustn't forget one of my largest treasures, grandchildren galore who seem to like me . . . a lot! I think that must be true. That's why they follow behind me at church and other public gatherings like little birds! I thank God for their presence. It gives me consolation and comfort and hope for moments and memories yet to come.

The most important thing I must include is the essence of life for me, the one thing I cannot do without: the presence of the Lord at every bend and bump in the road. How does one possibly make it any other way?

When I finish my lists, I'm swept by bittersweet feelings as I note how many of my memories fall into both halves of the page. I'm not exactly sure where some of the things go! I keep erasing and moving memories back and forth from top to bottom, for most of the painful stuff has elements of joy, sunshine, or comfort. For instance, it is hard to think of Tom without intense pain deep inside me, a pain that is almost unbearable. But it is also hard to think of him without basking in the flood of sunshine he brought to all our lives. I am smiling one minute and tearful the next. Some days I like to reflect on the thought that Bob and Tom might be making a perfect garden together in heaven and enjoying long talks and walks with each other that they never had a chance to have on earth. Then I remember, it doesn't really matter which list most of these are on. In my quiet time, I can still hear Bob's words: "He is the God of the top list and the God of the list at the bottom!"

This morning, as I look outside and see those little birds lapping up that water and hear their sweet voices lifted in praise and thanksgiving for the rain, I am reminded once more: I am not in this black night alone. The same God who has always come to my rescue has not gone away. He holds me during the dark memories and dances with me as I rejoice in the good ones. This comfort lets me cherish both lists and allows me to look forward. I drink in these moments of the past and they fill me up—giving me sustenance for the days to come. God reminds me: "Take those memories and use the strength they give you to live the moments you have left, Peggy!"

And so, like the birds who fill their bellies with the sweet drops of rainwater, I drink up these memories and go on. And as sure as the sunshine comes after the rain, He does restore my soul, and the joy of living in the moment is returning. Maybe the reason little birds drink so heartily is that they already know about this process of restoration. Too bad it takes us humans so many decades to understand the same thing!

> He never said you'd only see sunshine,
> He never said there'd be no rain,
> He only promised a heart full of singing
> About the things that once brought pain.
> Give them all, give them all,
> Give them all to Jesus,
> Shattered dreams, wounded hearts, broken toys;
> Give them all, give them all,
> Give them all to Jesus;
> He will turn your sorrows into joy.
>
> —PHIL JOHNSON AND BOB BENSON,
> "GIVE THEM ALL"

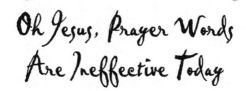

Oh Jesus, Prayer Words Are Ineffective Today

—Gloria

Oh Jesus, prayer words are ineffective
  today.
They float like dead leaves on the surface
  of the river.
But my prayer is in the depths;
  my prayer is drowning on the bottom.
Hardly a bubble of living breath
  is reaching the surface.
So God, articulation is out of the question.
Were Your words true when You promised
  to articulate for us at times like this?
Can the Spirit actually turn my throat-
  wrenching groans
    into something You can hear?
Can Your great heart reverberate
  to the quivering vibrations
    of my panicked heart?
Because one thing is certain:
  my groanings cannot be uttered.
The circumstances won't allow them to be.

And I can't translate this pain into words
    anyway.
I groan.
Like an injured animal my spirit groans.
Can You take my raw groanings
    and make a prayer of them?

The Only Thing We Have in Common
Is Our Use of Big Words

—Sue

Not long ago, I ran across these words to a very old song:

Brother, [Sister!] let me be your servant,
Let me be as Christ to you.
Pray that I may have the grace
To let you be my servant, too.

We are pilgrims on a journey, brothers, sisters on the road.
We are here to help, encourage, walk the mile and bear the load.

I will hold the Christ-light for you
In the night-time of your fear,
I will hold my hand out to you,
Speak the peace you long to hear.

I will weep when you are weeping, when you laugh, I'll laugh with you.
I will share your joy and sorrow till we've seen this journey through.

That pretty much sums up relationships! It doesn't say "if you are just like me" or "if you go to my church" or "if you wear big earrings and I don't" or even "if I have an impressive vocabulary and use big words and you don't." It says we'll do whatever it takes to see this journey through! As Bill Gaither says, "Good or bad, we've decided to go the distance with each other."

I think you can safely say that Gloria, Peg, Joy, and I are committed to going the distance with each other and—heaven help us!—carting up all our baggage (both the emotional and faux-leather kind) and dragging that along too! In sharing our journey, we seem to be proclaiming the same ole messages over and over. The first is, of course, that the four of us are very different, and if we had let those differences get in the way, we never would have known enduring friendship.

Second, we're vulnerable with each other. In other words, how can I possibly "hold the Christ-light for you in the night-time of your fear" if I don't know what your fears are? And while the song doesn't say this, how can I possibly understand if I don't listen? In this section, you'll read a prayer Gloria has written about listening. Listening not just to words but to the vibrations of the soul.

"I will weep when you are weeping; when you laugh, I'll laugh with you" rings true with us. We've done our share of weeping. I hope you'll hear my tears for Peggy in my chapter "I Know There Are No Simple Answers." In Gloria's prayer thanking God for friends, she says, "And when we become depleted in our sorrow, a friend will take up the slack."

Laughing is what we do best, of course. You'll find a lot of that in this section. Friends do poke fun at each other! Let me tell you about Joy's lists! And her friend Fyodor! And let me tell you about Peggy's whining.

Friends love recalling fond memories. In her chapter "The Best Things in Life," Joy points out that those best things seem, more often than not, to happen with a best friend. In "Pooh and Me," Peggy is Joy's ever-lovable teddy bear. (Wait! I ask you. Am I not cuddly? Is Gloria not teddy bear material? Is there more written about Peg in this section than both of us put together?)

Speaking of Peggy, she has taken this opportunity to compare people she's known with artichokes. Artichokes? (Can you believe she eats them out of a can?) And in another chapter we find out she thinks the reason we look so good to each other might be ... well, I won't give it away. Read it and find out! It's profound!

Gloria gives us a whole new perspective on relationships in her piece about the future. She got it from hanging out with the ... surely not! ... could it be? ... the *coroner?* I suppose coming from a small town, she doesn't have a lot of people to choose from. Still, the coroner? Puh-leeze!

By the way, did I mention how important humor is in a relationship? And did I mention how different we are but how much it actually enhances our friendship? And even our ministry? As I was saying to Gloria the other day, "Your laconic eloquence, Joy's tabula rasa writing style, and Peggy's and my soi-disant eclecticness provide the reader of our books with an olla podrida of good reading."

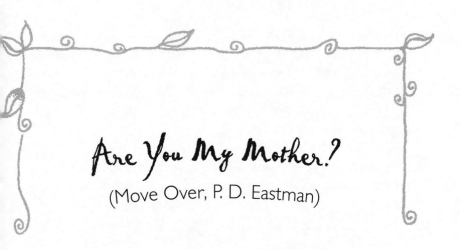

Are You My Mother?
(Move Over, P. D. Eastman)

Being short and scrawny has its drawbacks. It causes problems for me if I don't get to public gatherings early enough to get right up front where I can see. And I spend a lot of extra time and money on clothing alterations. I have enough pieces cut from the bottom of skirts and slacks to make a king-size quilt. However, the biggest problem concerning my size comes in dealing with my friends. Especially the three friends whose names appear on the cover of this book. Just because I'm short, pint-size, and look as if I have melted and run down in my boots, these three women think they should get to tell me (the senior member of our group) what to do. Not only are they free with advice for my life, they try to tell me when and where we are going and what we are going to do when we get there and even suggest what I might want to say when I get there! Honestly, they get on my nerves. They act as if I don't have sense enough to come in out of the rain! It's hard to always keep my good attitude and sweet spirit, but I do the best I can!

For over thirty years, Gloria, Joy, and Sue have played a major role in my life. Because I've been alone for so long, they have become a large part of my support system. They seldom forget to include me in their plans, and if they do, I just gently remind them! (This works well for me!) I think they think I'm their little mascot! Since it means so much to them, I have decided to go along with it. Anyway, it gives me almost constant attention—and gifts. And I do love the gifts!

I thought it might be fun to let our readers in on some of the dynamics of my relationship with these three. Each of them has brought special gifts to my life, and they offer me, through their uniqueness, bunches of fun, more free advice than anyone could remember, and rich blessings! Confidentially, what I'm going to tell you is sort of secret stuff. Shh! Okay, okay ... quit begging; it's not becoming. You can each tell one person!

What do I say about Gloria? Even though she is the baby of our foursome, she is my idea of the mother figure. She lets me be a little girl again. Just seeing her gives me comfort and solace. She's a shoulder to snuggle against ... a calm, peaceful resting place when I can't take the craziness of life. Gloria seems to be equipped with radar and to know exactly when I need to hear from her. Maybe it's a mother thing! We have been friends close to thirty-five years and have faced a lot together. I have figured out, without her telling me, that she has signed up for the long haul. When I am at her house, she makes me breakfast (boiled eggs, toast, fresh fruit, and great coffee). She buys me little surprises and sends me books and vitamins in the mail; she thinks I don't eat right! What a treat to get a care package from her! She forces me to see the big picture and helps me stay together by allowing me to fall apart occasionally. Okay, I'll confess (if I don't, Sue will tell it anyway), Gloria allows me time to wallow in my discouragements and even lets me cry and whine from time to time. Once in a while, she gets a little bossy with me and lovingly gives me a kick, you know where, and pushes me out of her warm, cozy nest and says, "You can do this!" In short, her love seems to be unconditional. At least I think it is. But don't think I'll push it too far, 'cause I've got a good thing going!

I think she thinks she's my mother!

Then there is Joy. Her very name makes me smile. She has the face of an angel, though she is just devilish enough to be fun. We clicked from the moment we first met in New York City about thirty-four summers ago. We like the same things, and we think the same things are funny. Give us an hour, a day, or certainly a week together at the beach, and we are two happy people. If our children don't know how to find us, that's even better! Sometimes we talk constantly; then there are long stretches during which we just sit and stare. I'll admit that is a pretty strange phenomenon for us both, but just like Pooh and Piglet, we each like to know the other is near, even when we are quiet. In the same way I know I can count on her, she knows that about me. Trustworthy, kind, and thoughtful, she brings honor to her name.

Ever since she met me, Joy has been trying to educate me, and I let her because she does it well and is so proud of me when I finally grasp what I need to learn. She has been like a walking college to me. Don't knock it. I have never paid tuition! I know bragging isn't good but . . . I'm one of her best students! Joy teaches creative writing to high school students, and one semester, she invited me to become a member of her class so that I could learn some basic computer skills and improve my writing. I loved every minute of it. The kids were fun and interesting, and watching Joy in action was a real plus. Most of the boys in that class were athletes and took the class think-ing it would be easy. They were cute . . . but wrong! Joy is no pushover. I probably shouldn't say anything but . . . the guys really liked me . . . a lot! In fact, they wanted to have their picture made with me. So if you see a picture of a cute little lady in the middle of a bunch of good-looking high school hunks, it's sure to be me! It will probably be blown up to poster size someday and sold for big bucks!

Joy looks out for me, and vice versa. She holds on to my plane ticket and to the directions for where we are going, and I save her a seat on the plane and buy her bottled water and candy bars. She proofs what I am writing (and will probably proof this!) while I run her errands or clean up her kitchen. She shares her food, her vacations, her home, and her husband. She pushes me and pulls me and corrects my English. She always chooses me to be her roommate when we are traveling. Gloria and Sue can tell you why. I'm not a gossip! Often she gives me her opinion. And occasionally, the teacher in her makes her just a tad . . . bossy! But she would never say I whine! Complain maybe, but whine . . . no!

I think she thinks she's my mother!

What to say (in print) about Sue? Truthfully, there is a lot. But for the sake of her family, I will not tell all! My husband and Sue were, shall we say—close. Everyone thought it was because he liked her looks, and they were right—he did! In fact, whenever he saw her, he made a beeline to hug her. He had planned to marry a girl like Sue. A long, tall, wraparound girl, as he used to say to me. Boy, did he get fooled. He fell in love with a very short "slip of a girl." There is no explaining love! One of the main reasons he liked Sue was her sense of humor. She is quick-witted (not to be confused with dim-witted). Bob was quick, just as she is, and the two of them together could keep the room rolling in laughter.

Sue has provided so much sunshine in my life. There have been times when she has brought me back to living again because she relentlessly pushed me to deal in reality. Being the original "snap out of it" girl, she kept telling me, "Just deal with today; don't try to take on tomorrow." She is very good at needling me, getting on my case, and pushing my buttons. She doesn't gloss over stuff and tells me what I need to hear, not necessarily what I want to hear.

I remember times when the four of us were getting ready to speak on a weekend. The auditorium is full of chatty ladies. The pianist is already playing. The singers are ready to begin. It's time for me to get up in front of all these people and say something that makes sense. I'm sitting in the front row, nervous as a cat, trying to collect my thoughts and to pray. Gloria leans over and says, "You will be fine. Just be yourself and talk from your heart. Remember, I'm praying for you." Joy, on the other side of me, whispers, "I am so proud of you. Just take your time and tell your story! Remember, I am praying for you!" Sue is sitting down the row with two or three women who have never laid eyes on us before. She is already eating the fudge she hides in her purse for emergencies or when she gets bored. Leaning over these lovely people, with her teeth tightly clinched and pointing an exceptionally long fingernail at my nose, she says these words of encouragement to me, in a very loud whisper: "Remember . . . don't sniff, put away that hanky, be spunky and funny, and for heaven's sake don't whine!" What a blessing she is at times!

So I get up and try my best to do what she says because she is needy!

She needs to win!

She needs to be right.

She needs to be needed.

She needs to be (I hate to say it!) bossy!

It seems to mean so much to her to boss me that I just go along with her. But I have found out that if I do what she says and whine just the right amount, I can lay such a guilt trip on her that she will shower me with gifts. It works every time! But I'm never going to tell her.

I think she thinks she's my mother, too!

I guess the Lord knew I would need a lot of help! With this many mothers, who could go wrong?

I Know That Friendship Doesn't Come Cheap!

Just as I was leaving for the airport, the phone rang.

"When are you leaving?" Peggy whined like a four-year-old who wanted a new tricycle. She knew exactly when I was leaving, and I recognized that whiney-piney tone of voice she gets. *On guard!* I thought to myself. I knew this woman's tactics. After all, we'd been friends for thirty years.

"Right now," I say with urgency. "I'm ready to walk out the door."

"Bring me something." Does whiney come in degrees? I think it does!

"Like what?" I say, trying to hide my impatience. *She's so little and cute and helpless,* I think for the thousandth time.

"Well, where are you going?" she asks, her voice brightening measurably.

"Topeka, Peggy, Topeka. Is there something you want from Topeka?"

"Guess that rules out something with seashells," she guffaws with no trace of a whine at all. *She can turn it on and off like a spigot,* I think.

130

"Bye, Peggy, gotta go."

"Well, bring me *something*. It doesn't have to have seashells," she practically demands, the implication being that it's the least I could do for a friend. Then voila! The whine returns. Will she stop at nothing? "If you love me, you won't forget! *(pause)* Surprise me!"

Can you believe I was in Topeka for two weeks, and every single day, I was thinking of Peggy (I could practically hear that you-know-what voice), and every single day, I was looking for something to take her? What will it be? Something fun? Something silly? Something nice? I kept searching. Even in Walgreens I was searching!

At last I found it, and I knew she'd love it. In a cute little tucked-away-in-the-corner-of-a-strip-mall garden shop, I discovered a hand-blown glass chicken in the most exquisite of muted colors. An *objet d'art,* if you will. I could just picture it in one of Peggy's famous little groupings on her kitchen table.

The lady offered to wrap it, and I busied myself checking out the earring display once more. Much later, when I took the gift out of the bag to hand it to Peggy, lo and behold, tied to the box by a hunk of raffia was a big seashell! We howled.

Who says Topeka doesn't have seashells, and who says acting like a brat doesn't work for a grown woman?

By the way, I'm going out of town next week. Please don't tell Peggy.

And oh my! I just realized Gloria is headed for Europe. I have a phone call to make.

Pooh and Me

"Pooh, promise you won't forget about me, ever. Not even when I'm a hundred."

Pooh thought for a little.

"How old shall I be then?"

"Ninety-nine."

Pooh nodded.

"I promise," he said.

Still with his eyes on the world, Christopher Robin put out a hand and felt for Pooh's paw.

"Pooh," said Christopher Robin earnestly, "if I—if I'm not quite—" He stopped and tried again—"Pooh, whatever happens, you will understand, won't you?"

"Understand what?"

"Oh, nothing."

He laughed and jumped to his feet. "Come on!"

"Where?" said Pooh.

"Anywhere," said Christopher Robin.

So they went off together.

—A. A. MILNE,
THE HOUSE AT POOH CORNER

Christopher Robin and Pooh remind me a lot of Peg and me. We have that easy kind of relationship. I would be hard pressed to identify which of us is which; in lots of ways, petite Peg is such a natural for Pooh, but then I'm younger and the one with the honey habit. The point is that whenever one of us says, "Come on!" the other will likely answer, "Anywhere."

Peg and I talk about sharing a cottage on the sea someday—the ultimate geographic fantasy for our days on this earth. It could be a perfect union, we think. We've made a few trial runs, and even though we're both talkers and nesters, we do well at the live and let live necessary for harmonious double occupancy.

In this space between the dreaming and the coming true, however, there are days and weeks of time in which we are out of touch with one another. Most of these occur when she's off to one coast or the other with another "best friend"; okay, so truthfully, she's more often speaking somewhere or preoccupied with the needs of children or grandchildren. I suppose it is during these times that I am most reminded to pray for her. I feel strangely discomfited when I don't know where she is or when she is coming back; I hate it when I can't merely pick up a phone to tell her some great idea I just had. (Maybe the angst is that I'm afraid she'll forget about me!) So when I can't talk to her, I talk to God about her. And it's good.

"Anywhere!"

Peg would say that. I can count on it. But the abandon that I so cherish in my relationship with Peg is far outweighed by my relationship with a God who, even before I know that I need or desire His presence, is available . . . everywhere!

P.S. I wrote this piece on a night when I had automatically pressed the touch-tone buttons for Peg's number and then remembered that she was gone on one of those long, multidestination trips whose stops I hadn't carefully recorded. I was surprised and even slightly agitated at my unrest when I realized I had no way to get in touch with her. And I remember being swept by a wave of thankfulness for her presence in my life.

Twenty years earlier, I probably did not have as much need for knowing Peg's daily whereabouts, but neither would I have had time for such reflections. My priorities were different. My time was monopolized by preoccupations such as ladyhood, motherhood, and neighborhood. I was writing, traveling, teaching, and accommodating my husband's habit of providing a halfway house for hopeful musicians. (The ones who hoped they were halfway to celebrity!)

Now, with our families grown and demands of homemaking much diminished, I find myself rejoicing my soul in the company of my friends in a way that I would never have understood nor been able to enjoy so fully twenty years ago. The God who is everywhere is also right on time!

Lord, My Friend Is Depleted

—Gloria

Lord, my friend is depleted.
The day-after-day demands of caring for
   the man she loves as his health
     seems to crumble in her hands
     are sucking her dry.
Small victories, huge defeats;
   encouraging moments, discouraging days
     seesaw over the arched frame
     of her optimism.
But gradually the weight added
   to both ends of the teeter-totter
     has begun to cut deep into her spirit.
Hold her up, Lord.
Help me today to know
   how I can ease the load,
     maybe give perspective
      to what comes to feel like
       a win-lose situation.
Lord, some days it looks like a lose-lose
   prospect.
But we both know—and her husband,
   my dear friend, also knows—

that under it all it's really a win-win
   proposition.
Lord, death is not the problem.
It's the daily grinding away of the dying
   that wears our spirits raw.
Let friendship be a healing balm today.
Let us laugh; laughter heals.
Let us cry; tears bathe the wound.
Let us have good conversations
   about children, politics, travel,
      work, writing, speaking—
         good conversations about the stuff of life
            that diverts our attention.
Let us reminisce;
   memory gives perspective on the present.
Let us pray;
   prayer teaches us to relinquish control
      to the only One who knows
         where we're all going
            and how we should get there.
Lord, thank You for my friend.
Heal her spirit today.
Let me be the one to nurse her to wellness today.
Come, Healer of Spirits.
Make us both whole again.

It's All in How You Look at It

Most of my life, I've heard that being a "person of age" means that you get to say whatever you want, wherever you want, to whomever you want! I don't know who made up that rule, but it does seem like this devil-may-care approach might be fun. Sort of a senior gift to humankind. Having been around people like that, I've picked up some tips that I hope to abide by when I get old! I mean if I get old! I don't want to be a sour, stubborn, argumentative, judgmental old woman. A woman who has a look on her face that seems to say, "I want to see the manager . . . *now!*" I like to think I have learned a few important lessons about making judgments and exercising my God-given right to put in my two-cents' worth.

A movie I once saw told a story about some women who had known each other as neighbors most of their lives. Now, toward the end of their lives, they were living in the same apartment complex where their lives intertwined almost daily. This is the conversation that I remember. One of the friends was telling her neighbors how another friend had hurt and disappointed her. She was

137

angry and didn't know if she could ever be her friend again. Finally, one of the insightful honest listeners spoke up and admitted, "Maybe she has been hurt by and disappointed in us, too! Do you know what I've finally come to realize? Most of us look better if we learn to see each other with squinty eyes! None of us is perfect."

I have a tendency to guard my feelings. Especially if I've been hurt by someone's careless words. Once, years ago, a friend at a party hurt my feelings and said words that embarrassed me and made me angry. On the way home, I began to rant and rave and sound off to Bob.

I said, "Can you believe she said that?"

His reply is still quoted often by my friends.

He said, "Sure. How does she know what she thinks 'til she hears what she says?"

Often I am guilty of talking first and then consulting my brain and my heart. That is true for me and of lots of talkers I know. Having lived in a house full of children most of my life, I longed to be with adults who carried on whole conversations that weren't interrupted by little people. Just to go out to eat with someone who didn't wear a bib was a big deal to me. So when I got around adults, I went a little crazy! I was a regular Chatty Cathy.

Bob, a man of measured words, said, with a twinkle in his eye and a grin on his face, "Maybe you should learn how to knit, so you will have something to think about while you talk!" While he was recovering from my socking him in the jaw, I was forced to consider what he was really saying about the damage we can do without meaning to.

Squinty eyes . . . I like that phrase a lot! Come to think of it, most people look better in soft blurred candlelight. And most of us could use a good airbrushing! No one does and says the right thing, the right way, at the right time all the time. But I'd like to think, in these years of living alone and having more quiet time to reflect, that I will do for others what I hope they will do for me: to see and accept without judging, not to impose on others what is right or wrong for me, to put myself in another's place, to walk beside them even if I can't walk in their shoes, and to just love them the way they are.

Last week, I picked up my new trifocals. Now I can hold a book comfortably in bed and be able to see to read. I can see the computer screen better, thanks to my new computer glasses. From my pew on the third row of the sanctuary, I can make out the preacher's face and a few of the old familiar faces in the choir. I'd like to add just one more adjustment to my vision list: to see others with the eyes of my heart and treat them accordingly, even if I have to take off my glasses and squint!

Lamentations of a "Best" Friend

Since this book is all about progressions through the seasons of life, and confessions of friends who have weathered so many such seasons together, I thought it might be appropriate to include a graphic example of the kind of interrelational dynamic that inhabits this fearsome "through thick and thin" foursome.

While I am at home in Nashville, composing nostalgic pieces like "Pooh and Me," sentimentalizing the long-treasured trust between best-friend Peg and me, she is off on a lovely October beach trip with her other best friend, Barbara.

She returns, rambunctious, brown . . . and bearing gifts!

Now, it is gratifying to know that she was thinking of me slaving away back here in a high school classroom, dreading the approaching cold, drizzly winter weather while she was strolling white sand beaches. But I wonder if there is anyone out there in Friendshipland who can appreciate my ambivalence about the state of this exemplary relationship when, documented in cold, hard print and painted pinewood, I learned just exactly *what* she was thinking as she purchased for me this extraordinarily imaginative "I missed you" gift: a sculpture of a dead blackbird, lying on its back, wire feet protruding straight upward from its inert body.

It is accompanied by a card that pictures the same dead blackbird, lying beneath a high wire on which sits a companion bird (I suppose the "best friend" of the deceased). The note reads: "Does this mean you will not be going south with me this winter?"

Need I say more?

Thank You, Lord, for Friends

—Gloria

Thank You, Lord, for friends.
Through the passages of life,
    good friends remain.
Through beauty and vitality,
        through the loss of energy and elasticity,
        through stellar achievement, and
            through embarrassing failure—
                friends remain.
Friends give when there is need—
    they celebrate and enjoy with us
        when there is abundance.
They laugh at our jokes and our foibles.
They cry at our griefs and at our sadnesses.
Friends pick up the pieces we leave,
    they take up the slack when we're careless,
        and they make up the difference
            when we come up short.
They listen when we tell them something . . .
    and they hear when we don't.
They love our kids, tolerate our dogs,
    and accept our spouses.

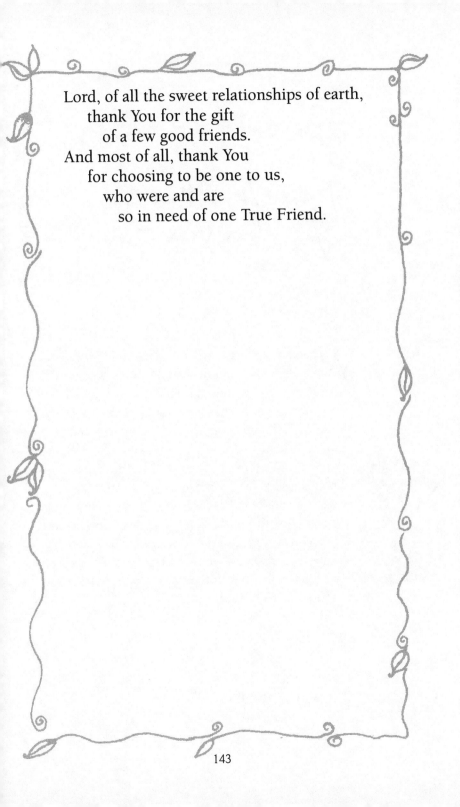

Lord, of all the sweet relationships of earth,
thank You for the gift
of a few good friends.
And most of all, thank You
for choosing to be one to us,
who were and are
so in need of one True Friend.

I Know It's All in How You Wear Your Hair

When I was a teenager, my friends and I flipped our hair this way and that, never quite looking each other in the eye. We moved from friend to friend. When my children were small, my friends and I still never quite looked each other in the eye. Our eyes were continually darting here and there making sure everyone was safe. We moved from friend to friend. The flipping days are long gone; the children are grown. My "now friends" and I sit for hours, drinking coffee, nibbling cookies, engaged in satisfying conversation. Sometimes we are silent. Now that I'm old enough to know better, I know we are such good friends because we look each other in the eye for long stretches at a time. I call us forever friends!

I Know That the Future Is Longer Than the Next Term of Office

It's election time and the streets of our town are lined with red, white, and blue campaign posters making promises, giving directions, and keeping names before the public. One in particular that I find amusing says, "Working for your future—John Carver for coroner." I don't think—were I a campaign manager—I would have chosen "working for your future" as a slogan for the office of county coroner. But maybe that's just because I'm not used to such honesty in politics.

I guess the truth is that the one thing all we voters have in common is a future that will one day be in need of the services of the county coroner. In fact, that office, perhaps more than any other, will come in direct contact with every one of us. After all, statistics do show the human mortality rate to be 100 percent. And while we like to tell ourselves that the coroner works for other people's unfortunate present, the truth is the "present" of

gloria

145

the six names in this week's obituary column of the *Times Tribune* will one day be my "present." So I can't help thinking that there are some things I need to do, not just on November 4 but today, this moment, to "work for my future" and the future of those around me—things like saying, "I'm sorry," writing a letter, taking in a lost child, lifting a load, encouraging my friend who is about to give up, saying, "I love you," hugging a widow, forgiving a transgression, making amends. Someone has said that dying is a process. I'm coming to believe the opposite: living is the process. Dying, once we figure out how to live, is no big deal. And the older I get, the more I am coming to believe that eternity starts here.

It begins when we choose to embrace the cross—the instrument of death—so that we can live in the resurrection mode. From then on, eternity comes into our days every time we give ourselves away for those things that last forever.

Today, "forever" came in the form of my little granddaughter Madeleine and the time we spent making chalk drawings on the driveway. Eternity was in the uninhibited embrace of the teenage boy with Down's syndrome I met at lunch. Life eternal was in the spontaneous singing around the harvest bonfire down by the creek after our family and friends had roasted hotdogs and bobbed for apples.

John Carver for Coroner— Working For Your Future

Tomorrow, "forever" may be making love to my husband, sewing a skirt for my daughter, or talking with a couple from Nebraska in our resource center. One thing's for certain, the only things that will survive this life are God's Word and relationships.

So come November 4, I, like my neighbors, will elect a county coroner. But I have a feeling what I do in the ballot box will not be nearly so important as what I do on the streets of our neighborhood after I leave the precinct station. I know for sure that my future will be much more secured by picking out a pumpkin to carve with Jesse, Will, and Lee, my three grandsons, than by choosing the best bronze casket in the county.

Sometimes a Story Is Just Too Good to Keep!

I was an only child for nine years, and so I spent a lot of time playing by myself in my playhouse under the hall steps. Upstairs I had another playhouse. The downstairs place was my home and the upstairs place was my business. Being an enterprising little girl, I had several businesses. One was a beauty parlor, as they were called back in the old days. I did my dolls' hair and talked to them the entire time. I paid attention to women's looks and suggested the "oh so fashionable trends" to my customers. I made up stories which I cheerfully passed on from doll to doll. By the end of the day, even as young as I was, I realized it's tough to keep every one of those stories straight, even if you wanted to . . . and I didn't!

Now that I'm older, I still have trouble keeping my storytelling under control. I can't remember from one day to the next to whom I have told which story when . . . or if I was supposed to tell it at all (whoops!). I love to tell stories; even if they are a little on the boring side, that doesn't bother me. My motto always has been, "There is nothing duller than a story with just the facts." I say, if you can't embroider a little bit, it's hardly worth telling! I can take someone else's story, and when I finish it, they will hardly recognize it. However, I know that attitude doesn't always serve the common good. So even though my gift is exaggeration, I do my best to refrain!

To this day, every time I get ready to tell someone a story, the thought crosses my mind, *Is this something that others need to hear, or should I just forget it?* Fortunately, at my age, forgetting it takes only an hour . . . or less! So if I can make it that long, I can control myself. It's not that I'm so holy; it's more that I am older and I like to think that maybe along with age, I might be getting wiser and more tolerant. My friend Barbara always says, "A word spoken can't be taken back." Think I'll try to remember that! Maybe that's what I should have told my dolls, but I'll bet you money that if I had, they would have changed beauty shops!

I Finally Admit That a (mumble) Makes Life Sooo Much Easier

(Don't Tell Joy!)

Shana, Joy's daughter, was precocious from the moment she was born, and because of Joy's busy schedule, Shana belonged to all of us. When Shana arrived, Joy was juggling more bowling pins than a circus clown. She was writing books, speaking all over the country to educators, and running a publishing company. She had other "full-time jobs," like entertaining Bob's business associates (usually with very little notice), writing songs for children's records, and nourishing family and friends. She did everything well. Thus, it wasn't unusual for Shana to spend the day with me—I was a stay-at-home mom at the time.

If ever there was a lesson for young mothers, it's how Joy raised Shana. Shana, who now is a rising young business executive, learned adaptability from the get go, and let's face it, you can accomplish most anything in life if you learn to be adaptable. Well, that and you have to make lists! Believe me, Shana learned that too. From the high mugga-mugga potentate of list makers. Her mother!

I often had Shana in the car with me while I was running errands. She would stand in the back and hang over the seat with her little curly head close to mine, and we would have a running conversation. (This was long before child restraints, of course.)

"Look in the sky," I remember saying to her once. "Look at the airplane. Look at the fluffy white streaks that follow the plane all the way across the sky."

"Aunt Sue, those are contrails," she replied in her sweet little eighteen-month-old voice. Yes, I wanted to tell her to stick a sock in it, but I thanked her profusely for articulating her concept so well and suggested she lie down in the seat and take a nap!

Another time she looked over the front seat and saw a paper with some writing on it.

"Aunt Sue," she said, "is that your list?"

Who but Joy would have an eighteen-month-old child who knew what a list was? Who but Joy would have a child as precocious?

I huffed and puffed about Joy's list-making for years. I teased her mercilessly. I even put her down on occasion. She always seemed to have one: in the front seat of her car, on her bedside table, on her kitchen cabinet, hanging from her nose, for heaven's sake!

Then one day I tried it myself; I made a list. And guess what? It changed my life. It simplified things. It helped me prioritize. I even bought tacky little printed pads with teddy bears on them and "to do" spelled out with gingham ribbons. Now I'm rarely without my list. Bank, cleaners, shoe repair, lightbulbs, overnight package to publisher, Victoria's Secret for leopard skin underwear, pick up chocolate, eat chocolate. But you should see my list disappear when Joy is on the scene. In the drawer it goes! In the glove compartment! Down the front of my dress! Wherever! I'd sure hate for her to know that after all those years of making fun of her for her lists, I now live by them.

I'm Not Afraid of Artichokes!

Yesterday I saw this headline in the living and style section of the paper. Martha [as in Stewart] says, "Don't Be Afraid of Artichokes." Sounded a little ominous to me, and so I read on. Until I was confronted by this article, I hadn't realized I should be afraid of artichokes. I'm not even sure of their origin or what family of vegetation they belong to. Are they fruit or are they vegetable? In all honesty, I've only tasted them straight out of a can, in party dip recipes or as a spread, served at most finger-food occasions I've attended. I have seen them in the produce section of the grocery, and I have admired them from a distance, for they are pretty and interesting to look at. Truth be known, I have observed them as maybe an object to be worked into a flower arrangement for Thanksgiving or Christmas. Eating one "in the rough" never even occurred to me. They're too much trouble. Like eating crab legs or shrimp that must be peeled, there isn't enough reward for all the time it takes to get at the meat. On top of that, I must admit they do look a little scary to me. Sort of foreboding; all spiky, prickly, and resistant to the touch. So I've just adopted the philosophy that if an artichoke doesn't bother me, then I certainly won't bother it!

I know people who come across that way. Attractive people who seem interesting from a distance but maybe just a little untouchable. They have a look that says, "Okay, you may look, but don't touch, don't question, don't try to get inside me where my life is really happening."

There is a man I know, who is married to a good friend of mine. I had never been around him much until she invited me to stay in their home when I was speaking in their area. I like her a lot and wanted to be with them and get to know him better. Besides, I don't turn down many invitations that close to the beach. I had always thought her husband just a little aloof, and I was concerned that it might be an uncomfortable few days for us all. I did know that he was smart, interesting, well traveled and well read and had a dry sense of humor, which is something I really like in a person. (I was married to the king of wry, dry humor, so I always find pleasure in it.) He is the kind of person whose brain you'd like to pick, or at least get a peep at his reading material. I'd seen him in public, and now I'd see him at home, and I wondered whether I would be able to peer inside the shell of privacy he guarded. My friend came across gruff, or maybe even harsh at times. I'd say he is a no-nonsense person.

I discovered after a few days that just like the artichoke, it would take a little work and time to peel away the layers. But beneath them was a very nice person, just a little shy and retiring. Underneath the gruffness was kindness, and underneath the harshness, I found fairness and honesty. And yes, he is Mr. No-Nonsense but all the while enjoys the humor of a situation. Quite often out of that gruff exterior pops a gentle soul, just an old comfortable "steel-wool teddy bear!" A little scratchy around the edges, but at heart, a compassionate, gentle spirit. I think his wife would agree. After all, they have been married about forty years. I believe she has decided to keep him. I imagine she feels like I do: there isn't enough time left on earth to train a new man in the way he should go! By the time I left their house and the beach, I had made a new friend!

I have discovered that people and artichokes have some things in common. The world is full of people who have much to offer my life that might make it more exciting if I can be patient enough and gently peel back the layers and be willing to risk a little resistance in the beginning. For hidden beneath those layers . . . who knows? One may find a wonderful surprise—the heart!

I think I may write to Martha myself! I'll tell her that most of her "tips and how to's" wear me out, but I'll thank her for the tips about artichokes and people. I wonder if she is smart enough to figure out what I'm talking about. I'll think about that and write her tomorrow. In the meantime, I'm off to the grocery. Just saw in the paper that they are having a sale on artichokes. I don't want to miss it! Artichokes today . . . and who knows, maybe persimmons tomorrow. Now there's a real challenge!

I'm Sure I'd Never Name a Dog Fyodor, Much Less a Child!

I would walk on my tongue before I would be sarcastic about my friends, but ... it seems to me that Joy and Gloria thrive like plants addicted to Miracle-Gro on their oh-so-intellectual authors and the books they write. For instance, the other day the four of us were together and they were discussing these two brothers with the bizarre name of Karamazaltoff or some such, and this other guy named Fyodor Dostoevsky, who wrote about them.

"Fyodor?" I said to Peggy, whispering behind my hand. "Give me a break."

"Sounds like the name of a stuck-up poodle," she giggled. "By the way, did you know the book they are discussing has seven hundred pages? *Seven hundred pages!*"

"*Single-spaced?*" I asked. "This is just my humble opinion, but I say a person is a lousy writer if it takes seven hundred pages to get his point across." At this point Joy and Gloria didn't have a clue we were talking about them, laughing at their expense. They were in their own little world, and Peggy and I were in ours—a better, brighter (albeit simpler) world, I might add.

154

"I've been meaning to ask you," I continued, "did you ever have any of those halcyon summer days that Joy writes about?"

"Well, if I did, I didn't know it." Peggy said with certainty. We both fell out of our seats laughing.

"What?" said Joy and Gloria in unison, spitting the word off their tongues like it was a fire ant.

Yes, dear reader, the four of us are very different! But friends we are! Forever friends! Forgiving friends! Through-thick-and-thin friends! And actually it works out quite well. When Joy and Gloria (who have degrees out the kazoo) get tired of intellectual pursuits, they can turn to Peg and me (Peg went from high school graduation to the delivery room, and I went to college to kiss boys) and say, "What's the latest from *People* magazine?" And when Peg and I finish discussing whether we think it's better to use oil or grease in our fryin' pans, we can turn to Joy and Gloria and say, "What's ole Fyodor up to these days?"

The Best Things in Life

The best things in life are those that cannot be named: those that create wonder, yearning, deep satisfaction, the feeling of a childlike joy so spontaneous that you have no idea what to call it.

At this past-midway point in my life, I am now arriving at the place where I can be wonder-full again and wise enough to know better than to try to analyze such moments.

How can you tell if you are there?

How long has it been since you giggled uncontrollably, unable to explain what was so funny?

Do you remember the last time you read something so moving that a lump welled up in your throat, brought tears to your eyes, and rendered you so inarticulate that you couldn't explain to a person occupying the same room what had laid you so bare?

When were you last awed wordless by a display of color, kindness, affection, or sound so glorious that it took your breath away?

Have you recently basked in the warm togetherness of two, in the same room, each engrossed in his or her own book or puttering about in separate, pleasant tasks?

Perhaps you have spent extended time in the company of a companion with whom you have experienced the ease of back-and-forth conversation—from the lightest jesting to the deepest or most intimate of things and back again—without the slightest adjustment.

Was it only yesterday you found yourself anticipating the return of someone dear with such intensity that upon their arrival, there was a great bursting of joy?

When was the last time you watched siblings in pleasant play, affectionate collaboration, or in tender protection of one another? And smiled?

Have you noticed how many of the above-mentioned moments happen best and most often with a cherished friend?

How often do you shiver with awe and gratitude at God's unconditional delight in you?

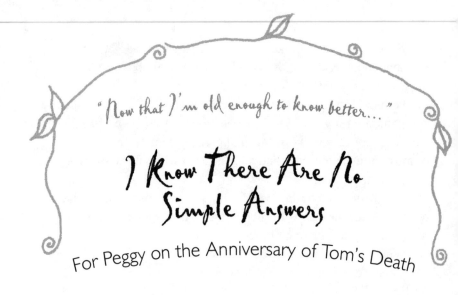

I Know There Are No Simple Answers

For Peggy on the Anniversary of Tom's Death

I understand!"

"You do?"

"I can't begin to understand."

"It's okay."

"He's in a better place, you know."

"I know."

"You have other children. And you have grand-children!"

"You're right."

"Talk about it, Peggy. Try to gain closure."

"Good idea."

"Don't talk about it, Peggy. Try not to think about it."

"Hmmmm."

"Spend time alone, Peg."

"I'll try."

"Try *not* to be alone."

"I'll try."

"Try not to mope, Peggy."

"Trying."

"Don't whine, Peggy."

"Sorry."

"It's been a year. The grieving period is over now."

"A year? Already?"

"Peggy, move on now. Get on with your life."

"What choice do I have?"

"You need to get over it, Peggy."

"Get over it? What about when a big ole pickup truck with the windows down passes me on the interstate, and there he is, blond curls blowing in the wind? What about when I'm quietly watching TV, and the handsome Tom look-alike on the glass commercial smiles out at me? And what about Tom's boy, the spittin' image of his dad; what about when he comes toward me up the walk? And on Sunday when they sing his favorite hymn, what about that? What about when I pick up a handful of rich brown dirt and feel his presence beside me in the garden we loved and worked together?

"Get over it? Get over it, you say? I don't think it will be soon!"

Whispering Hope

I woke up this morning humming "Whispering Hope." Where the quaint, old song came from in the storage bin of my memory is anybody's guess, but there it was, working its way to the surface of my consciousness as I opened my eyes.

It surprised me. I had gone to sleep somewhat discouraged with myself and by the expectations of others—not exactly fertile ground for hope. Besides, the old song itself had always seemed rather bland and shallow to me as a maturing young quester. Not enough edge to it, I thought; not enough content.

So I spent today revisiting those old lyrics and repenting for the hasty judgment of my youth and my lack of attention to what I now realize is a profound and life-sustaining truth:

Soft as the voice of an angel—
Whispers a lesson unheard.
Hope—with a gentle persuasion
Whispers her comforting word:
"Wait! till the darkness is over;
Wait, till the tempest is past.
Hope for the sunrise tomorrow,
After the shower is past."
Whispering hope. Oh, how welcome thy voice!
Making my heart, in its sorrow, rejoice.

A few months ago my friend Peggy lost her thirty-five-year-old son—a tall, handsome, funny, strong, outdoorsy young man who was about to "turn out." No one quite knows what happened, but what began as a hiking expedition into one of his favorite places in the hills of Tennessee turned into a nightmare. Peggy's son Patrick phoned her with the news that Tom's body had been found at the foot of a wet slippery cliff.

Bill and I, too, have a strong, funny, grown son who is as dear to me as Tom is to Peggy. I tried to imagine how Peggy would ever climb through the despair of such an unfathomable loss. I'm not sure I could. All the kind words, sympathetic letters, arms around the shoulders, assurances of continued prayer, admonitions to trust it all to the God who made us—all the good advice in the world—would not make it possible to crawl out of bed another morning and face another day full of other people's children and other families' joy.

Yet over these years since I first heard the song I woke up singing this morning, I have seen the amazing power of "the hope that is within us." I see it now in Peggy. And I am coming to know that some of the most quiet, unassuming truths are the most life changing and the most healing.

I am learning that hope cannot be conjured up by our will and grit. No, hope, like faith and love and patience and forgiveness, is a gift from God. As trite as this may sound, hope is more likely to wake us in the morning with the sound of whispering in your ear,

"Come with Me; you can go on!" Hope is a vision, a dream, an inspiration projected on the screen of the soul from somewhere else.

Joseph was a receiver of hope. Even though he was in the pits at the hands of his wicked brothers, hope gave him the dream of a transformed family who would one day love each other. Even when he seemed to be rotting and forgotten in prison, the dream film flickered on.

As a childless old man, Abraham was a receiver of hope so insistent that he spent his evenings building a baby crib and a high chair.

David was a receiver of hope. He saw projected against a night sky the dream that lifted him from the sheepfold and finally placed him in the palace of the king.

Mary was visited by hope, a hope so certain that she endured through the bitter reality of a bloody cross to an empty tomb and, finally, to a hilltop in Bethany, where she watched her Hope—and the Hope of the world—return to the God who gave Him.

Paul's encounter with hope was anything but subtle. It did not whisper in the night. No, his vision blasted into his swaggering misdirected self-righteousness with such a force that it left him blinded by its reality and struck dumb before its awesome revelation.

Hope—the fragile, gentle, whispering, tough, enduring, awesome stuff dreams are made of—is the gift of God to every fainting heart.

Return to your fortress, O prisoners of hope.

—Zechariah 9:12

Confessions about . . .

Perspective

I May Be from West Virginia,
but I <u>Have</u> Eaten Out

—Sue

When I was a little girl, I thought mashed potatoes were the only food group worth having every day, day in and day out. To me, mashed potatoes were the ultimate! Then I grew up. Became worldly wise. Experienced exquisite gourmet offerings from the five-star restaurants of such "food cities" as New Orleans, San Francisco, and New York City. I dined on the unique specialties of the ethnic neighborhoods of Montreal, Miami, and Chicago. I was privileged to travel to foreign lands and partake of the exotic delicacies therein. Now that I'm old enough to know better, I know that mashed potatoes is the only food worth having every day, day in, day out. Well, that and chocolate!

At least mashed potatoes is one subject the three of us, little girls at heart, agree on! Maybe the only one. And while the other three wouldn't stick their pretty little pearl-laden necks out so far as to say that chocolate is the *ultimate* food, I can tell you they'll clean me out in a New York minute when my back is turned!

In our first book, *Friends through Thick and Thin,* you, our readers, discovered how very different the four of us are. The way we dress, our likes and dislikes, the way we think. You learned we've not just accepted each other's differences, but we've celebrated them. Even we are still amazed at that after more than thirty years of friendship!

In this section of the book we call "Perspective," you'll find us quite opinionated in our confessions. Especially about things that don't matter all that much. Check out Gloria's chapter on bras, and Joy's dot-com-ments. Peggy speaks loudly when it comes to the subject of silence, but frankly, Gloria, Joy, and I haven't seen that side of her. And Gloria writes about running a marathon, but Joy, Peg, and I don't ever remember seeing her standing by the door without car keys in hand.

You'll find that, in many cases, we don't yet have a perspective on the subject we're discussing. Does that stop us? I don't think so! We just go ahead and worry the subject up one side and down the other and try to it figure out as we go. And we'll drag you along with us; there'll be five of us, instead of four. The more the merrier! You'll be party to our musings, like my story about a young classmate, and Peg's and Joy's entries that bare their souls as they search for an understanding of God's ways.

How many times have you been so crazed by the things going on around you that you'd like to change identities—become a different person altogether? Peggy's solution is to just get in the truck on one side and come out the other as somebody else. I know a good idea when I hear one!

A note before you begin: Have you ever played a game in which everyone is given a handful of pennies, and for the duration of the party, each time you say the word *I* you are penalized by giving up a coin? Let's just say that by the end of this section, the four of us will be out of pennies!

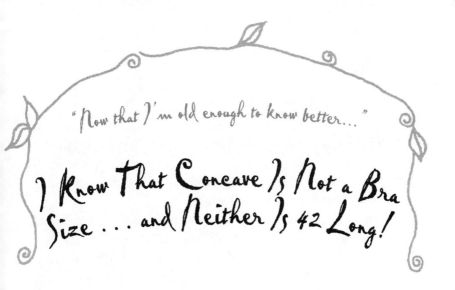

I Know That Concave Is Not a Bra Size ... and Neither Is 42 Long!

I developed early. By the time I was finishing my tenth year, I was five foot two and had a curvy body. By then, my oh-so-with-it mother had brought home a garter belt for wearing nylon hosiery (that was just before panty hose), a neat kit with sanitary napkins and all I would need should my menstrual periods begin, and three "beginner bras" marked 32AA.

gloria

The small protrusions on my chest really didn't require a bra to "give me support," but the bra gave me some protection from getting bumped playing kickball in the schoolyard. That was reason enough for wearing what amounted to little more than a band around my chest, since my "breasticles" were as sore as a boil and so sensitive I cringed if anyone even passed me in the hallway.

And I had hope. My hips were rounded, my waist was narrowing, and there was every reason to believe that, given time, my sore spots would blossom into a real bustline. I waited.

And I'm still waiting. I really don't think it is too much to expect that with all the estrogen that has coursed through this body for close to five decades, I would at least be able to graduate beyond training bras. But alas, the truth is I still can use my bra for a purse, since there is always plenty of room for a couple of Kleenexes, my hotel key, spending money, a notepad, and anything that doesn't create too obvious a lump.

Since fifth grade, my body (and my overall bust measurement) has expanded and contracted many times. Let's just say my husband has slept with women of every size and never had to leave home to do it. My closet rod should have those little plastic rings that say 6, 8, 10, 12, 14, none-of-your-business.

But the cup size has fluctuated all too little. At my heaviest and as a nursing mother, I managed to actually fill a B cup if I had the necessities of the day stuffed in there to round things out. The rest of the time the excess cup space just hung there like a deflated balloon because manufacturers have taken it upon themselves to mandate that if I measure thirty-eight inches around the bustline, I must, of necessity, be more than a size B. God forbid that I should ever grow to be forty inches around the chest! I'd have to resort to carrying produce in my bra.

And forget that pretty, delicate lacy underwear! That is made only for infants thirty-two inches around or less. And the fabric they allot to go from bra cup to fastener must be two inches wide max. Any soft female tissue attached to a woman's rib cage just has to hang over like the belly on a Sumo wrestler hangs over his thong.

My friend Sue, who before her reconstructive surgery following breast cancer used to make Dolly Parton look like a peer, tells me the problem is just as difficult on the other side of the standardized norm. I wouldn't know about that. She had to battle stays that won't stay and underwires that puncture a lung if you give them any unexpected maneuvers. By the time the generous bustline has lost its elasticity, you're too worn out to hassle the manufacturers anymore. It's just too much trouble to keep up the crusade to make whoever surveys the "demographic" come to grips with the fact that demographics don't wear bras.

But there is hope. A new generation is emerging that still has a voice. And I am optimistic when I pick up the charts and find that enough of these women have made a national hit of Trisha Yearwood's song "Real Woman"! And it makes me admire Jane Russell for beating the system by having Howard Hughes design her a bra of her own. At least one woman walked this earth in comfort, and that gives me some self-respect, if only vicariously.

Point and Click

A n insert in a recent *McCall's* magazine offers the twenty-five best websites for women. They are neatly categorized under the following headings: Shopping, Beauty, Health and Fitness, Family, Pets, Food, Career, Money, Home and Garden, Travel, and Entertainment. (I wondered if those were in order of importance.) Just point and click, and a life well-ordered, organized, prioritized, etc. is laid out before you. Little muss or fuss.

Point and click.

You can have lunch in the office or evening's dinner delivered wherever you are; enter your address to find restaurants nearest you.

Pick a movie you have loved, type in its title, and a website will give you a list of similar choices; saves you the trouble of reading reviews, back liners, or discussing with your friends their favorites.

Get advice about pets without addressing either a pet, a vet, or another pet owner.

Click www.___.com to send an electronic greeting card in which you have made little sacrifice of time, energy, or money. You have to travel no farther than the distance between yourself and your computer. You don't have to stand while you read the dozens of choices, nor hunt for the right size envelope, a pen with which to address it, or a stamp of the proper denomination to carry it to its destination.

The recipient will experience no heart palpitations waiting for the mailman, nor any suspense at approaching the mailbox, but next time he or she logs on to e-mail (most often improperly, carelessly written e-mail), a pleasant, mechanical voice will announce, "You've got mail!" The subsequent ninety-second interlude of advertising and unsolicited extraneous information, never mind the intrusive porno lures, is hardly a heart stopper. Just one click and all the obligations and experiences are over. The recipient has been properly Happy Birthdayed, congratulated, whatevered! No envelope to toss into the recycling bin, no display space needed on the mirror, coffee table, or dresser. No nagging need to add another treasured piece of memorabilia to the scrapbook. Click! It disappears. How neat! How nice!

Click! I'm now going to leave my computer desk for a while and pull out the big cardboard box from the bottom shelf of my closet. I just want to touch all those lovely cards I've received over the years from dear friends who chose to give me the immeasurable gift of their time and energy—expressions of their hearts and souls, expressed both in fragments of borrowed sentiment and in their own eloquent or stammered thought. Each one signed, stamped, and delivered by human hands, occupying a place of honor until it gathered an appropriate amount of dust; then it was filed away for a rainy day or a surprise future moment.

I may even get out my treasure chest of old love letters from Bob—the ones he wrote when he was in basic training at Fort Dix, New Jersey, and I was teaching school in Orchard Park, New York (a million miles apart then). And he was desperately lonely and I was starry eyed, butterfly hearted, and tingly all over at every charming, eloquent word of his broad scrawl on that square white paper.

There is a phenomenon in that process that will never be a memory of today's young courtiers … or is it my aged mind that can't quite picture that the same kinds of dreams can be engendered by the hurried messages of e-mail, fax, and digital beepers? It seems that compassion and intimacy just don't translate as well in abbreviated language.

Of the gaggle of gadgets birthed to make our lives easier in the last decades of the old millennium, perhaps the most celebrated is the one on which I type these words. I must admit I enjoy its efficiency (when it works), but I lament the price paid in intimacy; in the beauty of a child's labored scrawl or a grandmother's perfect Palmer penmanship; in a former pride invested in the written language, now abbreviated to the point of mutilation (much to the expressed sorrow of aging English teachers); in the tactile joys of textured papers and colored envelopes decorated with smiley faces or an SWAK; in the privilege of lingered response.

Point and click. It's quick. But it leaves a kind of lump in my throat and a sad little space in my sixty-some-year-old soul.

P.S. Here's a laugh! The spell check on my brilliant, state-of-the-art computer brings up the word e-mail, offering me only these choices: Emil, remail, mail, and em ail. The status notification says questionable spelling. Ha! So much for modern technology. It seems to be confused about itself!

I Don't Always Know Who I Am ... but He Does!

My grandson is Britt Benson-Greer. When he was born, his mother, Leigh, was in graduate school and so I had the joy of his presence almost every day for the first two years of his life. His animated face and big blue eyes could totally capture me when he talked to me. One dared not look away or try to think about something else while he had the floor. His expression seemed to say, "Pay attention. There will be a quiz on this information later."

Through the years, Britt has maintained this attitude, and he has a vivid imagination to go along with it. His lively imaginative powers have given birth to some great adventures, of which the following story is a perfect example.

One early spring morning, Britt, his sister Annie, and his mom were out in the yard. Leigh was trying to get some weeding done before the weeds took over her perennial flowerbed. Meanwhile, the children and their imaginations were busy at play. Out of the corner of her eye, Leigh saw Britt open the door to the red Ford truck. He picked up his straw farmer hat from the front seat and a piece of two-by-four plank, which he pushed down the

173

back of his jeans, causing him to hold himself quite straight and erect as he walked across the truck seat and got out on the other side. He walked around the truck toward his mom in a sort of stiff, straight, all-business manner, with just a touch of good ole boy and a slight strut thrown in for good measure. His hat was tilted to the side, and he kicked at the dirt with a dusty cowboy boot as he extended his hand to his mother.

"Howdy, ma'am. My name is Mr. Flattback. I've come to fix your television. Mighty nice place you have here!"

Leigh thanked him.

"How many acres ya got?" he asked.

"Sixty," she answered.

"Is that so? Got any kids?"

Before she could answer, he quipped, "Well, you aren't paying me to talk. I'd better get to work! Now where is that television?"

There have been many days when I would have liked to do what Britt did that day—get in a truck on one side and come out on the other as someone else. There were days in the course of my life, primarily since my husband died, when I got up and realized that my life lacked focus. Even at this tender age, I sometimes catch myself thinking about some new thing I'd like to learn or something I would like to do, and it hits me . . . a voice somewhere inside pipes up and says, "Peggy, if I were you, I'd get on with it! You're no spring chicken! You don't have that many years left. Especially, if it involves bending over and getting back up!"

I hear a lot these days about finding oneself and about knowing who one really is. I wonder . . . if I could figure out who I am and what I am really about, would I like the person I have become?

When I look in the mirror, whom do I see? It's a question I have thought about more specifically since I have lived alone. Bob and I knew each other intimately. We could anticipate each other's reactions and could finish each other's sentences. We even stole one another's punch lines! We were so intertwined that when people saw one of us, they asked about the other. Words were not always necessary between us, for I knew without a word what he needed to say. I felt his touch even when he was across the room from me. During those last years, we cried together and laughed together and found out our sense of humor was our salvation. We were able to put into words the hopes and fears that two people who have loved each other for a long time share.

At the time of his death, when I looked in the mirror, I saw Bob. I had become so attuned to his needs. After a few months alone, I discovered that I had known Bob much better than I knew the Lord or even myself. Here I was, on my own at fifty-two. What was I going to do? What was I going to be, now that I was "all grown up?" No babies to rock, no meals to prepare, no one waiting for me to come home.

Deep inside, where no one sees but the Lord, I began to hear Him speak my name. He reminded me that the answer was in me! Planted there long ago! He knew me in the womb! And I remembered His promise. I am not alone, for He walks with me on my journey! "For you created my inmost being; you knit me together in my mother's womb. . . . My frame was not hidden from you when I was made in the secret place. When I was woven together in the depths of the earth, your eyes saw my unformed body. All the days ordained for me were written in your book before one of them came to be" (Ps. 139:13, 15–16).

He had been waiting for me all along to get in the truck and come out on the other side as myself. Not Bob Benson's wife or Leigh's mother or Britt's gran. And He keeps showing me that as I know Him more, He will teach me to reinvent the self I need for each day. He will give me new direction and new work to do. After all, I am His child!

Fourteen years have passed since I began my "journey of intimacy" with the Lord. The gift of His presence and the opportunity to speak and to write about my experience has been the glue that has held me together. What a relief to let God be in charge! I have a new goal these days. He has planted within me a deep desire to live so close that I will be able to look in the mirror in the morning and see Him in me! On a day when I have lost my focus and the assurance of what I'm about, I am thankful that I need no imaginative powers or a truck to walk through to know who I am in Christ. "Stop dwelling on past events and brooding over days gone by. I am about to do something new.... Can you not perceive it?" (Isa. 43:18, 19 REB).

> I can't find the see of it,
> but I feel the pull of it.
> Only God knows the where of it.
> I know Him ...
> So I am sure of it!
>
> —JAMES D. TAYLOR,
> "THE FUTURE"

I Know That Freedom Is More Than Fireworks over the Ocean

F reedom is not enough. Free for what? I couldn't escape the question as I enjoyed the spectacular fireworks display with my family. My grandchildren's faces were alive with wonder. Their excitement spilled out in oohs and ahs and astonished expressions.

But after our senses had been saturated, even fireworks bored us. We had declared our freedom. We had celebrated our freedom. We had made explosive and bombastic statements into the sky about how very free we were. But we, like the rest of the cheering audience, one by one folded our blankets and lawn chairs and disappeared into the night and would soon forget why we came, unless we did something with our freedom.

I am reminded of an incident that happened when our now-grown daughter was about four years old. She had seen the Statue of Liberty, and we had explained to her that it stood

gloria

for freedom, welcoming all who came into this country from places that didn't offer the liberties we all take for granted. One day she saw on television the statue of *Venus de Milo*. With a stricken look on her face, she came into the kitchen where I was working. "Mother?" she asked. "Is Liberty dead? Without arms, is Liberty dead?"

As we celebrate our country's history, I am surrounded by a generation that does not remember a world war or even, for the most part, the Vietnam War. These kids have never seen a ration food stamp or stood in a soup line. Even as a parent and now a grandparent, I do not remember the Depression. So it is easy to take for granted our common freedoms. And because we take them for granted, we fail to see caution lights flashing in our minds when freedoms begin to erode.

Politicians make declarations. But declarations are not enough. Applications are demanded—quiet, daily, simple, practical applications of freedom. We are not freed to strut; we are freed to love, to serve, to move where the tides of need pull us, to go where the winds of hope blow us.

As the last sparks of fireworks fell into the ocean with a sizzle and a puff of steam, the masses left to return to their dark and temporary dwellings. For a while they would talk about the fireworks of freedom. They would discuss which expressions they liked the best—the round orange ones expelling purple stars, the shooting comet ones that whistle and bang, the unity fires that rise simultaneously into the air like a bouquet of lilies, then peel off to do their own thing.

Then there would be no more to talk about. Conversations would dribble off into silence. Hope and expectations would dissipate, too, like the fog after the sun burns through, searing our faces with the harsh and brazenly glaring reality of empty hearts, empty hands, empty promises. Fireworks are to celebrate freedom, and freedom is for doing. We are free to do something heroic.

Perhaps without wars and depressions to define *heroic* for us, we will be free to define it in better ways than carrying a buddy with a blown-off leg back to the foxhole. I've actually seen this generation contribute some very exciting new definitions.

There was the teenager in the paper last week who gave a kidney to save her mother's life. And how about the six-year-old who had the presence of mind to call 911 and calmly give his address to the police when his mother fell down the basement stairway and broke her leg?

How incredibly heroic it was of a woman scientist who was given less than preferential treatment to take simple corn and use it to identify DNA, a discovery that will change all of our lives—and perhaps our whole trial system—forever.

Yes, child, without arms, liberty may well be dead. Our arms. Our hands. Our brains. Freedom is for doing something more than holding a torch to a Roman candle and watching sparks fall into the ocean. It is for igniting the fires of the human spirit and lighting up the world—or at least our personal piece of sky.

"Now that I'm old enough to know better..."

I Know That "Red and Yellow, Black and White, All Are Precious in His Sight," Even Means a Green Person

When I was a child I learned a little song: "Jesus loves the little children, all the children of the world. Red and yellow, black and white, they are precious in His sight. Jesus loves the little children of the world." Missionaries told us about children with red and yellow skin, so even at quite a young age, I could grasp the concept, even though in my world everyone was pretty much just like me. I knew there were families with more children than ours, that some daddies didn't have as good a job as our daddy, that some parents didn't make their kids obey like ours did, which we knew, of course, was for our own good.

I knew early on that half of all people were Catholics and half weren't, since that's the way it played out on my street. When I was Mrs. Vandertweezers, all dressed up in my mama's discarded clothes, I was invited to have tea with the nuns at the convent, and yes, there was something slightly mysterious about Catholics. But we were all human beings, for heaven's sake!

As to skin color, again, I only knew my own neighborhood. I thought it my lucky day when the elegant, black uni-

180

versity professor who lived next door (in a bigger house than ours) let me make a playhouse on her porch. Even better was to be invited in, to be included with the pretty black students who came to study in the parlor.

Then one day I met someone really different. I was in the first grade and it was the first time it ever dawned on me that not everyone was just like me. Several months into the school year, in the middle of the day, the principal walked into our classroom holding the hand of a little waif of a boy with an ear-to-ear grin. "Class, this is our new boy. This is David Latlip. He'll be with us for . . . a while."

Skinny! Scrawny! Taller than every other kid in the class and probably a year or two older. David was different. Different from his slick black hair, with the grown-man haircut, right down to his—also grown man—wing-tip shoes.

"He's green," I thought secretly, and my song certainly didn't account for Jesus loving green children. Today, years later, I can still see those olive-colored hands: pristinely scrubbed and seemingly connected to little tributaries of "clean" that made their way through the arm grime and disappeared behind the rolled-up sleeves of a stiff-as-cardboard, laundry-starched, white-as-snow shirt. As the days passed, the laundry-starched shirt went from stiff as cardboard to limp as a rag; from white as snow to grubby; from grubby to dirty, and eventually to filthy.

"Part Gypsy," the teachers whispered as they speculated on his uncanny dark looks: his black eyes, and his greenish skin. David's dad was the owner of a traveling carnival, the most run-down little hand-to-mouth, two-bit operation of a street carnival imaginable. At the time, it seemed pretty glamorous to us! David was what was called a carnival kid. His mother was dead.

When the carnival was in town, David was in school. Two months here, three weeks there. He would appear seemingly out of nowhere, sometimes in the middle of the year or in the middle of the day, and a party atmosphere would prevail, if only for a moment.

"Oh David, you're back," the teacher would say. "We've missed you! We were just going over our spelling (or history or math);

here's a desk. Barry, share your book. Sharon, give David a pencil and a piece of paper." He would settle in quickly and once again be one of us. Well, not quite one of us, because not only did David dress differently but his home life was different.

Most of us went to our pretty little bungalows with cozy front porches with gliders and swings and rag rugs, to mothers in pretty pinched-in-at-the-waist cotton housedresses, and the smell of dinner cooking on the stove. We sat down at dinner tables with freshly ironed tablecloths, with brothers and sisters, and a daddy who loosened his tie before he said grace.

David went home to a rusted, beat-up little one-room trailer that sat lopsided in a gravel and sawdust parking lot. He went home to a communal dining arrangement shared with a motley crew of misfits that included showgirls, sideshow freaks, riggers, ticket takers, and cotton-candy makers. The fare was a one-dish meal of who-knows-what prepared outdoors in a gigantic, beat-up, not-too-clean kettle by a sweaty fat man in an apron that displayed recipe ingredients from days, maybe years, gone by.

Sometimes when called on in class, David would answer with a swear word, and the rest of us would suck in our breath and our eyes would pop out, but the teacher never got mad. For anyone else, it would have been a week without recess, a phone call to our mother, and then heavens knows what! Somehow it was understood that in David's world, swearing was an acceptable answer. Later the teacher could be seen alone with David speaking quietly. After that, for a while David would catch himself before saying the forbidden words.

Despite our differences, David was our friend. Somewhat of a celebrity! Probably because he knew so many things the rest of us didn't and had seen so many things the rest of had never even dreamed of. For instance, he knew what was behind the canvas sign that proclaimed "Side Show." He knew the bearded lady and the alligator man personally and claimed to have held a two-headed baby in his arms.

David had seen a naked woman! In fact he had seen more than one naked woman, and with words, he could paint the picture so vividly the other boys could pass on the description like it was firsthand. He had a lot to teach us, but he knew to pass along his information sparingly. In a way, David was already a carnival man in that he knew he had to keep 'em coming back.

Eventually David disappeared from our school lives. One day he was there, and the next day he was gone. Several years passed, and we were visiting family in the Upper Arlington area of Columbus, Ohio (Upper meaning upper income in most people's minds). At the time, my uncle was president of the largest bank in town, and he and his family lived next door to the governor. We had been out to Sunday dinner—all dressed up, daddies in suits and ties, mothers in gabardine two-piece dresses, and the children in their best—when we spotted a carnival. After a bit of begging on the part of the children, the parents agreed to stop. We paid our admission, bought our cotton candy, and were just making our way to the merry-go-round when I heard my name. Sure enough, there was David smiling from dirty ear to dirty ear and, as my mother described it later, happy as a little lost pup. My guess is that David hadn't had a bath since the last time I'd seen him, and I'm reasonably sure he was wearing that same once-white shirt.

I was thrilled to see him—I could barely contain myself—but by this time, I was well aware that knowing someone like David could work against me in high society. Perhaps I missed the whooshing sound of relatives sucking in their breath at the sight of David. Perhaps it never happened. What I do remember is this: my parents treated David with great honor and respect. They asked about his life— we were on his turf, after all—and made him feel important.

To this day, I can never pass a Ferris wheel without thinking of David and wondering what became of him. It's

183

been almost half a century since I last saw him, but I can picture him like it was yesterday. Sometimes I sing the song: "Jesus loves the little children. All the children of the world. Red and yellow, black and white . . . and greeeeen!" "Green" I sing at the top of my lungs and hold it a few extra beats, which of course throws the meter out of whack. "Jesus loves the little children of the world."

I Know That We Are Fearfully and Wonderfully Made

When the psalmist said we are fearfully and wonderfully made, he was right on! Our bodies are a marvel. Oh, I know all the typical examples: the five senses, the digestive system, the miracle of reproduction, all the big stuff. But the details are what truly amaze me. Supposing, for example, that when women carried a baby, the "bundle" were not nestled in the cove of our pelvis, centered side to side and top to bottom, but planted under an arm where, as the baby grew, the weight would make us list like a ship whose cargo had shifted in a storm. Or suppose we carried the baby on our hind end or between our shoulder blades; we either couldn't sit for nine months or would get reverse curvature of the spine.

Supposing our joints were fused and immovable. Forget crawling, running, or trying to get up from sitting or lying down. Marriage proposals and prayers would have to find a whole new posture. Humiliation would need a new symbol.

Aren't we thankful, too, that our necks can turn? How would we ever back out of a parking space at Kroger without risking an insurance claim or a lawsuit? And how would we ever know what our kids are up to in church or what our friends are doing behind our backs?

Have you ever stopped to think what a blessing it is that God made the cleavage in our buttocks run up and down and not sideways? Think about the embarrassing panty lines that would cause! And how mortifying would it be going down the slide on the elementary school playground with our "cheeks" flapping like a baby's lips making "raspberries"? On those days when I'm tempted to demand more miracles from God, I just stand in front of a mirror after I get out of the shower and say instead, "Never mind. Miracles never cease!"

Silence Is Not a Bad Word!

I've taken a lot of kidding in my day about being such a talker. When my friends at my home church ask me what I do when I'm gone on weekends and I say that I speak, their response is always the same. "That's no surprise!" or "Boy! Are you in the right job!" When I remind them I also get paid for talking, they usually start laughing so hard they have to hold their sides. Can I help it if one of my most outstanding attributes is the gift of gab? I quickly let them know that when one is invited to speak, she is actually expected to say something (especially if she is paid) and, furthermore, is expected to say something that makes sense. So it isn't that easy! Talking is one thing; speaking is another. Pardon me for bragging, but possessing both the gift of gab and the gift of exaggeration, I can pretty much talk to anyone anywhere on any subject. And I pretty much do!

My children have a large array of vacation pictures of me talking to strangers in airports, hotel lobbies, and restaurants. One I especially remember was made in Switzerland on a ferry crossing to a small island near

Lucerne. In the background are the lovely Swiss Alps, covered in snow even in July. Am I looking at the Alps? Of course not! I am talking to these people on the boat as if they were old friends. Never mind the Alps. Never mind I will never see them again. What is truly astounding is the fact that these people don't speak English! Not to worry; it didn't bother me one little bit. I still had fun talking!

I've often heard there is a lot to be said for silence. Frankly, having been married with children most of my life, I can't say I've had much experience with it. I've always operated on the theory that there is a lot of air and space, and someone is gonna fill it up talking, sooo . . . why not let it be me?

My husband was a quiet, shy person who really had a lot of good stuff to say. He also had a wonderful sense of humor with impeccable timing. My job was to listen to what he was whispering in my ear and then to say it out loud. Sometimes I even got credit for his funnies. It took people a while to realize that he was the funny one in our family, and also the profound one! Being the extrovert that I am, I enjoyed the publicity while it lasted.

Over these past few years since he died and all the children grew up and left for their own homes, I have lived alone. Having never been alone in my life, this has been a rude awakening for me! I am learning about silence. I need it and value it. I've made peace with it. Silence has much to teach.

Not long before he died, Bob told me a story. He was speaking somewhere but was not feeling all that well and could hardly wait to get back to his hotel room and rest. He sat down on the edge of the bed and, without even thinking, flipped on the television just in time to hear a preacher who was recounting a conversation he had had with God. The preacher had been ill and had gone to the doctor, who said that he needed to stop talking and rest his voice for a year. If he did keep talking, he would probably lose his voice permanently. And now he was on TV saying to God, "I don't have time to be sick! There are people who need to hear what I have to say, Lord. You must heal me . . . now!"

Bob said he could just imagine God thinking something like this: *I had planned to say some things to you while I had you still and quiet before Me, some quiet, tender moments just for us to share, but I can never get you to stop long enough or be quiet long enough to hear Me, and so it's just easier to heal you and let you go on your way and miss the fellowship of the silence.*

Often, when I catch myself scrambling to find my niche in the body of believers, I am suddenly reminded of that story. How often do I miss hearing the Father because I'm so taken up in my own notions of God's work? How many times has He struggled for my attention, only to be denied it because I'm so caught up in some newfound church program or speaking opportunity or maybe something really important like making a marriage work, guarding a friendship, or caring for my children? All of these efforts may have great value, but only if He whispers His approval into them. I'm not exactly the smartest kid on the block, but I do know this: God does not scream at me; He quietly and patiently waits for me to be quiet before Him and listen for His dear voice.

I wish my friends and my family could know how much I've come to treasure my silence. I have heard more in thirteen years of quiet than in a whole lifetime of noise! It has truly become my refuge and my fortress. A place where I lay myself open to Him and His will, where I find strength for my journey and hope for the days to come.

However, once I'm refueled and out the door . . . look out! I can talk you under the table, whether I know you or not. It really doesn't matter. As my friend Champ says, "I don't know anything about it, but I'd be glad to talk to you anyway!"

I Know That This Race Is Not a Sprint but a Marathon

When I was in the Burlington, Michigan, elementary school, we had what were called Field Days. The whole school was involved, and we could sign up ahead of time for the field event for which we felt most suited. There were the standing broad jump, the running broad jump, the high jump, the discus throw, the relay race, and the 100-yard dash. Maybe there were more events—I don't remember.

gloria

I wasn't very athletic. I couldn't even throw a softball well enough to make the girls' summer team, so discus throwing was out of my league entirely, and only tall girls with long legs seemed to excel at the 100-yard dash. But I always tried the running broad jump and the high jump. For the broad jump, someone stood at the side of the sawdust pit to mark and then measure how far from the jumping line one landed. More graceful, stronger kids always beat me out in that one.

The high jump was performed by jumping over a cane pole resting on pegs in two parallel vertical posts. The slightest touch would dislodge the pole. The object was to get a running start, then hurl one's body over the pole. Each successful try was followed by the official moving the pole up one more increment on the posts. The long, lean type was always superior to me in that event.

You can understand, then, why the metaphor of a race has not been the scriptural comparison to most inspire me. A wave of fifth grade nausea always seemed to swell in my stomach whenever I read Hebrews 12 and felt Paul start in on me as a runner and the spiritual journey as a Field Day event.

But now that I'm older and wiser, I am coming to believe the race so often referred to in the Bible is not a 100-yard dash or a broad jump (running or standing) or a high jump or a discus throw. I'm coming to believe that these verses aren't even about winning. The race, I am discovering, is not a sprint; it's a marathon. And the object of this life event is to *finish!*

It doesn't matter whether I run, jog, or eventually manage to drag my pulsating, throbbing body over the finish line. The point is to finish, to get there without quitting. I'm coming to see that whenever I think I can't go another inch, there is a support team running alongside to catch me when my knees buckle. There are fans in the bleachers all along the well-planned and chosen course that have long since found this race possible by finishing it themselves. At every bend in the track, there they are, cheering and encouraging at the top of their lungs. "Yes! You can! You can make it." In the body of Christ, that's what friends are for.

And I am—finally— coming to know that endurance is what the Coach is after. He's not interested in spurts of flashy athletic prowess. He isn't impressed by sleek bodies, rippling muscles, or perfect physiques. It's determination He adores. It's the earnest pursuit of the goal that makes Him proud. It's the beauty of the gift of commitment to the experience itself—staying the course, keeping the faith, and enjoying the journey.

The trophy is engraved not with "First Place Winner," not with "Most Valuable Player," but with "Faithful until the End." I, even I, can sign up with confidence for that. I may not be good, but I can be stubbornly persistent to the end.

Lord, You Are Teaching Me the Importance of Finishing the Race

—Gloria

Lord, You are teaching me the importance
   of finishing the race.
I've never dwelt much on sports
   metaphors;
I'm not much of an athlete.
I'm so thankful You didn't say "win the
   race," but You did say "finish."
Lord, life is full of times it would be easier
   to drop out, to be the runner left behind,
      injured or exhausted at the side of the road
         while the surviving pack leaves you
            to eat its dust.
But this race is not a sprint;
   it is a marathon with varied terrain
      and twists in the trail.
The point is to finish.
How encouraging it is to know that the
   great apostle Paul summed up his life
      in terms not of "winning"
         but of finishing the course, endurance.

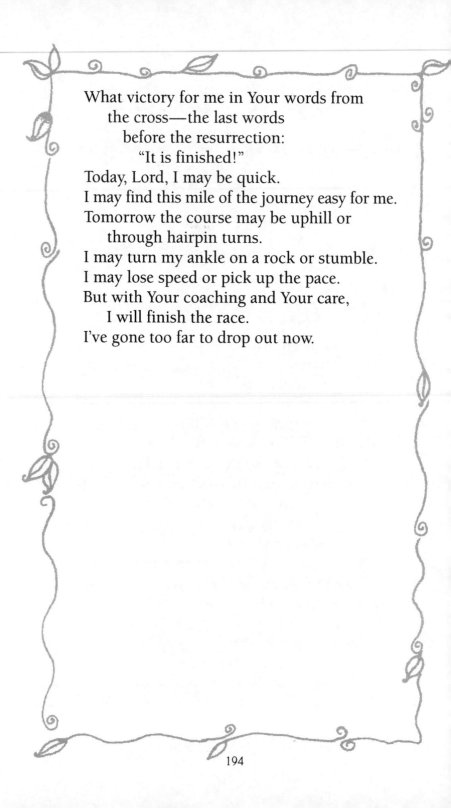

What victory for me in Your words from
    the cross—the last words
      before the resurrection:
        "It is finished!"
Today, Lord, I may be quick.
I may find this mile of the journey easy for me.
Tomorrow the course may be uphill or
    through hairpin turns.
I may turn my ankle on a rock or stumble.
I may lose speed or pick up the pace.
But with Your coaching and Your care,
    I will finish the race.
I've gone too far to drop out now.

I Know It's All in How You Tell the Story

Have you ever noticed you can take a story and color it to your advantage? You can make it either positive or negative depending on how you report it. Here's a good example. It's not unusual for those of us who live life on the road to entertain each other with horror stories of being stuck in remote airports for six months with no food and water, or for showing up at a speaking engagement in Paducah and finding that your luggage is in Tacoma, and that you've spilled a plate of spaghetti down the front of the outfit you're wearing. It's a "can you top this" kind of thing.

When I boarded my plane in Grand Rapids, Michigan, it was with great satisfaction. The reason for my filled-to-the-brim feeling wasn't necessarily because my friend Mary and I had just pigged out on a mega-giga breakfast, although that helped! We'd had omelets with everything but the kitchen sink, fried potatoes piled to our chins, toasted English muffins gushing butter and jelly, and as if that weren't enough, we decided to share a pecan roll—a pecan roll so big it made our eyes pop out, not to mention our tummies.

My cozy feeling was also the result of a visit to Zondervan Publishing House. Secondary to Mary being my friend, she is my editor for children's books, and she had presented me with the finished art for my book *Mudpie Annie*. The colors were so beautiful I just wanted to lick the page. Well, not really, but you know what I mean!

The night before, I was guest speaker at Mary's church for a women's event, and I'm not bragging, but it was a great success. I can't even take credit (but of course, I will) because undoubtedly these gals would have had a great time whether I showed up or not. I don't remember ever having such a good time with a bunch of women. I'm talking the kind of women you just can't get enough of. I wanted to hire a bus and take 'em home with me!

My success story had taken a turn by the time my plane arrived in the air over Chicago, and after having to circle an hour, I missed my connection. *Oh well,* I thought, *there are plenty of flights to Nashville.* But when I checked with an agent, I found that the 3:00 flight was canceled, the 6:30 was full (I could stand by), and the soonest I could be sure of a seat was 9:40. Wow, would I have a sob story to tell!

I was looking at ten hours in a crowded airport full of whining kids, businessmen screaming into cell phones like banshees, and disgruntled people banging into my legs with carry-ons. No food, no water (I didn't even have my laptop, for heaven's sake!)—except for Fannie May Candies, of course. I bought a pound and called my husband.

"Put your stuff in a locker and get on the train," he said. "You don't even have to go outside; takes you straight downtown. Three bucks round trip. Take a cab to Greek town; eat at Costas (our favorite Greek restaurant); say hi to Eddie (our favorite waiter). Don't sit in the airport all day. Go shopping!"

Wait! Did he say shopping? I barely said good-bye. I became a whirling dervish, gulping my Fannie Mays, stashing my briefcase, breathlessly running for the train as though it were the last train outta Dodge (and as though they didn't run every six minutes). The rest is history, as they say.

The question is, How do I tell my story? Do I go for the sympathy vote? "Wheew! This life of travel can get you lower than Filene's basement. Let me tell you about my six months of torture in Chicago. Do you know what O'Hare airport is like when flights are backed up? Whining—no! make that screaming—kids, businessmen howling into cell phones like banshees, and disgruntled people practically amputating legs with their carry-ons! No food, no water! And to think! All that to speak to women who didn't even need me?" Or do I tell about the unexpected, rejuvenating bonus day, truly a gift from God in the midst of my busy life?

As I said before, now that I'm old enough to know better, I know it's all in how you tell the story.

I Still Don't Get It!

Most of the time, I am trying to understand what God is up to! I tend to want to get inside a problem and try to solve it. Like the way I read a mystery novel, spending so much time trying to find a solution that the whole point of enjoying the story is lost on me. Surely there are other people like me! The kind of people who have inquiring minds that want to know! Folks with a real thirst for knowledge, who really need to know what's going on. Surely I'm not the only one who is nosy!

peggy

This process of trying to understand what's happening in my life and how I should react is once again my current task. Do I have a clue about what the purpose is? Not one! But I do believe that God speaks to His children through the passages of life and that it is important to share these passages with fellow strugglers. There is friendship with the Father available for all. He is with me. His very presence gives me hope. I wish the answers came easier, and yet I would not want to miss the light and warmth of His presence as we walk the journey together.

It seems to me that part of this "night of the soul" struggle is learning to handle it on a daily basis. Do I scream and cry and clench my teeth and tighten my grip? Do I shake my fists at heaven and cry out, "I will survive"? After all, I am a woman, and women do know how to survive. Is that defeating the purpose God has for me? In the process of being a tough, emotionally strong woman, am I missing a more important lesson? The Bible says that it is in my weakness that He gives me strength. Maybe I should back up and start again. Instead of trying to figure out the end of this mystery story, maybe I should trust Him and enjoy the unfolding saga of daily life. After all, that's really all I can do. So I am trying to quit stewing over the "past or last" pages of my story and concentrate on the now and what my role in the process should be.

I used to worry about being called to speak. I never dreamed I would have an opportunity to speak and write from my heart. I feared my lack of education might cause someone to be wrongly influenced. I've discovered, though, in these last years, that folks really don't care about my education or lack of it. They aren't bothered by how many honors or certificates or diplomas I don't have on my wall, how many books I've written, or how many hundreds of people I have spoken to. What they are interested in is my life experience and how it might relate to their own. And so I lay myself open on these pages, and this is what I'd like others to know about me: I, too, have been broken. I have tried hard to listen to my life and to let Him speak to me through it. Even in the stillness of the midnight, when I reach out, He pulls me toward Himself. He offers to me once again life, hope, strength, comfort, and oh yes . . . grace and mercy! I am so thankful for grace and mercy!

Do I understand? No way! Furthermore, after following Him for almost fifty years, I still don't get it! Do I trust Him with the comings and goings of life? You'd better believe it!

Be still, and know that I am God.

—PSALM 46:10

Day by day, and with each passing moment,
Strength I find to meet my trials here.
Trusting in my Father's wise bestowment,
I've no cause for worry or for fear.
He whose heart is kind beyond all measure
Gives unto each day what He deems best,
Lovingly it's part of pain and pleasure,
Mingling toil with peace and rest.
Every day the Lord Himself is near me,
With a special mercy for each hour.
All my cares He fain would bear and cheer me,
He whose name is Counselor and Power.
The protection of His child and treasure
Is a charge that on Himself He laid.
"As thy days, thy strength shall be in measure,"
This the pledge to me He made.

—CAROLINA V. DANDELL-BERG AND OSKAR AHNFELT,
"DAY BY DAY"

A Wish for the Journey

Sunday, June 11, 2000. Two days ago a friend faxed us this quote from a Brennan Manning book:

> May all your expectations be frustrated, may all your
> plans be thwarted,
>   may all your desires wither into nothingness . . .
>   So that you may experience the powerlessness and
>   poverty of a child,
>   and sing and dance in the mystery of God.

Yesterday I spent most of my day working on my part of the manuscript for this book, which is due to the editor next Thursday. I labored especially over two pieces. "Old Dogs . . . New Tricks" was about becoming older and wiser—wise enough to be firmly committed to "Show me your ways, oh Lord; teach me your paths." The second was "Losing Is Better Than Winning," in which I talk about what I had learned through experiences of great adversity and the blessings that always accompany suffering and sorrow.

Today as I awoke, my husband was making his way rather shakily through our bedroom toward the hallway. I sensed something was wrong.

"I have a little problem," he said. The eternal optimist, he always underestimates problems. "I have lost the vision in my good eye; I can see only shapes and light in the other with the detached retina."

The whole story is much too long to tell, but the short version is that after several years of dealing with the ravaging effects of diabetic retinopathy, advanced heart failure, and a hastening deterioration of general health, which has included many surgeries, hospital stays, and medical emergencies, we have in the last three months been greatly encouraged by a very successful cataract surgery and by the discovery of a new noninvasive treatment program that could possibly restore some life energy to the heart and kidneys.

The doctors had proclaimed that they were clean out of tricks, and we had thought that there were no more medical miracles to be expected. Then out of the blue, through no effort of our own, we suddenly had access to several kinds of new information that brought us fresh hope and a renewed spirit.

The journey to this point has indeed been one of blessing beyond anything we could have dreamed, but the events of this day bring us to yet another of those losing places Brennan Manning would wish for us—smack dab back in a position of powerlessness and poverty and with another chance to "sing and dance in the mystery of God."

It is noon now. My singing voice is clearing a little, and I am frantically looking for my dancing shoes! The journey continues . . .

Islands of Faith

There are islands on this island. At this resort, Bill and I seldom hear or see anything God-aware. We are almost never recognized. For the most part, this island is populated by coastal peoples: east coast, west coast, Florida gold coast. Most are not even aware of the Great Plains and the Great Lakes, let alone the sea of God's great love. Yet this morning, trying to find a place of solitude, I slip into a small hidden cafe in a historic old house just off a downtown street. I hide at a small table in a corner and order fruit and coffee, though I have had my break-fast. I want to write, be alone, and think.

Suddenly, I am aware of voices famil-iar to me and unfamiliar to this island. Someone is singing, "I wanna live like I'll be leaving today." The lyric catches my atten-tion. I listen to two or three more songs as they come up on the CD player somewhere in the soul of the house. The voices are from young

gloria

people I know—Steven Curtis Chapman, Ce Ce Winans, 4-Him. They sing things like "we can work together," good, society-friendly songs. Until I became aware of "Jesus, have mercy on me."

The plate under my scone says "The Quaker House," and the singer is singing, "Jehovah, Prince of Peace . . . in the presence of the King."

I look at the name of the place—"Kendricks'" at the Quaker House. Who are these Kendricks people who have dared to create this island of faith in this sea of secularism and affluence? The place, like most here, is simple, sparse. I notice an abstract metal sculpture on the wall. Now I realize that it is a cross on level ground. There is a sort of upside-down staircase at the opposite end of the ground from the cross; a figure clings precariously from the vertical line of the tallest step. I want to ask about the sculpture, but I also want to remain anonymous.

I keep my silence in the corner and instead just give quiet thanks for this oasis island. I am renewed by the anonymous fellowship. It is enough.

This Island's an Arsenal of Memories

—Gloria

Lord, this island is the arsenal
    of so many memories for our family.
Good joy-filled days of summer,
    melancholy days of autumn,
        passages of our lives,
            stages of our children,
                chapters of friendship—
these have been marked and celebrated,
    closed and mourned,
        recalled and revisited here.
This year, the theme song of my heart
    is gratitude.
I am thankful for it all
    and for the years and experiences
        that have given me perspective.
Islands—especially this one
    with so much history of its own—
        give me perspective.
Islands are apart, separated by space, sea,
    and refreshing breezes from the network
        of mainland demands.

From them a sense of priority emerges—
    an overview of all that pushes and
        shoves us around on pressured days.
Thank You, Lord, for islands,
    and for this one in particular.
Teach me.
Show me.
I thank You for all I see from here today.

I Know That God Can Handle Things without Me

(Who'da Thought?)

When I was young, I was taught that it was up to me to tell the world about Jesus. Somehow I thought that if I didn't evangelize every living soul on earth, it would never be done. Now that I'm old enough to know better, I know that God doesn't need me one little bit. He doesn't need me to write books or speak at conferences, witness on airplanes, or even give money. God can do His work all by Himself, thank you very much! Knowing that means I can take a deep breath and relax. The monkey's off my back. NTIOETKB (Now That I'm ... you know!) I know that while He doesn't need me, He wants me! He wants me to part of His plan and His process for making Himself known to the world. And guess what? When I'm part of His plan, I am the richer for it.

Mind Wanderings — or Wonderings — on the Subject of Celebrity

(At This Age, the Two Words Are Nearly Synonymous!)

I often find myself walking around some public gathering of Christians or gospel music fans with Gloria, and it feels a lot like following Minnie Mouse around Disney World. Everyone smiles, speaks, wants to touch, get an autograph, or at least tell her how much her last song or book or video was loved. Gloria wears that kind of recognition well—with patience and kindness—and away from the fans, it never occurs to her that she is something any different from the rest of us. She is happiest on her own back porch with a cup of coffee, and she'd sit there and talk to anyone who's interested in words, birds, trees, bees, books, country living, or one of her four grandchildren.

The celebrities in Peg's life are children—anyone's. Walking with her through a supermarket, a mall, or an airport is always an occasion prolonged by her pausing to admire or speak to anyone under three feet tall. Perhaps it has something to do with her own petite frame; I don't know that she has ever observed a child who didn't captivate her.

Then there's Sue. Sue presupposes that everyone she meets is a celebrity and often mimics the likes of one herself.

At airports, she has been known to greet strangers with open arms as they arrive at a gate. In our travels, we have left multiple limousine drivers and convention hosts waving good-bye to us tearfully, confused as to whether we or they were the VIPs. Every one of them was holding Sue's e-mail address.

Sometimes I wonder whether we have become real people people or whether perhaps we are just jaded, having spent so much time around well-known public figures—at least those of our own subculture. We aren't very taken with celebrity. I'm not sure what kind of extraordinary being it would take to impress us.

Personally, I can't think of a person of world renown for whom I would go far, pay dearly to see, or faint dead in my tracks upon contact with, though there are many for whom I have high regard and would enjoy observing or engaging in conversation. Am I weird or what?

Once as I watched the Gaither Homecoming group of friends singing enthusiastically "Soon and Very Soon, We're Going to See the King," I entertained the private concern that even heaven might be less impressive to someone whose pulse is not quickened by things like royalty and the crown jewels. (I did once stand in line over two hours at London Tower to see both, and I decided I liked my grandmother and my own thirty-dollar pearl necklace better.)

Will I be impressed with the Heavenly King? I have little doubt that the answer is a clear affirmative . . . because going to meet *the* King is not about celebrity. Oh I will see my real self as the pauper and Him as the ultimate ruler, and I will be breathless. But because I am finally of His mind, I will be seeing this relationship not in the context of commoner trembling in the presence of superstar but in the light of redemption. I am here at His invitation—chosen by Him. He gave up His notoriety just to get to know me. How can I not be impressed?

Oh yes! I will be overwhelmed—not with so great a celebrity but with so great a love.

I Have a Good Rememberie!

My granddaughter Annie often comes and spends a day or two with me. I love to have the children one at a time. When you have fourteen grandchildren, this is called brilliance! They grow so fast that if you don't take the time to dote on them now, your chance will be gone overnight. If you have several children at once, the chances are you will wind up being taxi driver, doctor, mediator, activity chairperson, and short-order cook. I like to give a lot of attention, one on one. Besides, when you have just one, you can find out "stuff" that is going on at home without appearing to be nosy. Sometimes that backfires, however, and you find out more than you really wanted to know!

Annie was at my house a while back, and we were playing games she brought from home. Games she had learned how to win! The game she chose for us to play is called Memory! I knew the minute I saw the name of it that I was in big trouble. You look at all the cards face up, and then turn them over and try to remember which card matches which picture. Every time we played, Annie beat me fair and square.

I finally said, "Annie, you are so smart. How do you do that? I can never remember all of those. There are too many different pictures."

Annie rolled her eyes at me, thought a minute, and said, "I guess I have a real good rememberie!"

Some days I think, okay . . . this is it! I knew sooner or later it would happen. This is the day. It's gone! (My mind, I mean.) There are times when I don't know where I am going, and for the life of me, I cannot remember where I've been, much less what I did while I was there. I just pray that it was legal!

A "rememberie" is a wonderful thing. I often have to flex my "memory muscle" quite vigorously to get it moving. Lately, the circumstances of my life have caused me to do quite a bit of remembering. When I reflect on my journey with the Lord, I find great strength in recalling a series of glorious intrusions He has made on my life.

First He made me a part of a church family where I could come to know Him. The most important choice I will ever make was deciding to follow Him. When I was young, I watched people who were my parents' contemporaries live out their lives. I'm not sure at what point it dawned on me, but eventually, I realized they had what I wanted: His constant presence in my everydayness. Choosing to welcome Him into my heart has been the basis of all I have done in life. And He reminds me that He chose to live in me!

How blessed I have been with His gifts! The gift of good friendships is one I especially hold dear. I have counted quite heavily on friends. How do they seem to know when I need them? Are they magic? Out of nowhere, they come by bearing gifts, just like the wise men! Often they call or send a note. Sometimes they get lax, and I have to call them and whine a little and refresh their rememberie. Friends have given me the gift of celebration; even when I don't feel like it, they force me to party anyway! And He chooses to come with me to the party!

I find that life is a little tricky at times. One of the problems with remembering past moments is that the good and bad are all mixed up together. Some moments are so wonderful, the joy can hardly be contained, and some are bittersweet and bring a tear to the eye and a lump in the throat. And still He chooses to be present! Through the good stuff and the bad, His presence is the one essential I cannot live without. He lives in me!

Perhaps the most tender and intimate of His intrusions are those during which He calls me to prayer. I have never been accused of being a prayer warrior! My usual "M.O." is to not call on the Lord until I am hanging by my fingernails. If you could see my nails, you would know this is not so good! Often I pray in such desperation that I'm sure He must think that I think He can't remember without my constant reminders and nagging. One minute I am asking Him to help me hold on; the next, I am begging Him to help me let go. Sometimes I am so busy telling God what I think that I really don't listen. I ask Him to be God in my life, then I tend to tell Him how to do it! I am trying to learn how to best hear His call to pray, understanding that I am just a novice. He gently reminds me, "You did not call Me, I have called you!"

Now that I am old enough to know the value of intangibles, once again I've set out to follow Him with the same reckless abandon I had as a teen, not having a clue about life. Thankfully, I made up my mind, oh so long ago, to follow Him wherever He might lead me. What a journey! What blessed gifts my Father's intrusions have been.

My memory is fading a little these days; in a way, I am grateful. It helps not to remember the pain so vividly. But Annie, I want you to know, I do remember the good stuff; I remember it well. I guess I have a pretty good rememberie too!

Here are some words I hold dear in my rememberie:

For one reason or another I am not always a follower. Sometimes I am afraid to go. Sometimes my life is so good that I do not want to leave where I am. But when I have gone and when I have allowed it to become my word, I want to say to you unreservedly, *wherever is worth going*. At times I have remained behind only to find myself surrounded with nothing. But sometimes I have also left all to go with Him and I have known His everything. And I am convinced if I would always go I would always be glad.

The quest—
    Wherever it takes you—go;
Whichever the task—do it;
    Wherever the burden—accept it;
Whenever it calls—answer it;
    Whichever the lesson—learn it;
However dark the path—follow Him,
    Because wherever He takes you,
        It is worth it.

—Bob Benson,
Quest of the Shared Life

Lord, Sometimes I Feel Guilty for Being Still

—Gloria

Lord, sometimes I feel guilty for being still.
My soul feels small and shriveled;
    I know I need to stop—
I need to center my mind, my emotions, my
    plans on You.
Yet when I save time to be quiet before You,
    when I stop the motion
        and find a place to listen,
            I feel guilty.
I have been too conditioned
    to gauge my worth
        by what I am getting done
            instead of on what
                You have already done.
Lord, this pressure to accomplish something
    is felt even more in those circles where Your
        name is used freely.
"What are you doing for the Lord?" seems
    to be the important question—
        spoken and implied.

But my spirit tells me that these are
    human expectations, not divine ones.
What You want is relationship with me.
Lord, I am here today to enjoy You,
    to be with You,
        to listen to You.
Would You take me into Your presence
    and wash away the earth
        from my feet
    so that I may walk into Your place
        without leaving dirt prints
            on Your carpets?
Let me be at rest in the silence.
I bring nothing—
    except my hunger
        and my full attention.

Confessions about . . .

Passages

Like Gloria Says, "We're Just Four Little Girls in Grandmothers' Bodies"

—Sue

 Age is something we'd rather not think about. Or talk about! Or write about, for heaven's sake! Although it's not like everyone on the planet isn't getting older. Everybody is! The four of us wrestled long and hard with how we'd address the A-word in this book, and we thought Peggy brilliant for coming up with the "now that we're old enough to know better" theme, and Gloria even brillianter for suggesting the little girl sketches. As for this section of the book, we first called it "Aging." That didn't last long; we changed it to "Growing Older." Quaint but not it. Finally we landed on "Passages."

Passages! That works! It sounds as though we're still in motion, which we are, and that we aren't yet ready to turn in our tutus and dancin' shoes. We'll even admit that the end may be in sight somewhere way off down the garden path, because we all know, death is part of life. The last part! I can't quite picture the four of us, in our sunset years, sitting on the porch sipping drinks together. If so, I suppose the drink would be Maalox! Peggy's with a sprig of mint in it. A Maalox julep? I mean really!

Joy's best writing is in this section of the book. I found myself sucking in my breath over and over as she contemplates change, wrinkles, brokenness, and heaven. Peggy, too, writes about

218

heaven, while my contribution is craziness as usual, but pay close attention to "I've Stopped Looking for That Perfect Age." Considering it was written by a shallow person, it's deep.

To the other extreme, Gloria—who in the introduction called us "four little girls in grandmothers' bodies" (don'tcha just love it?) and keeps reminding us how we've come full circle—is once again the anchor of the section. You'll find yourself reading her prayers over and over: alone, with friends, and aloud at public gatherings.

Lord, It's a New Day

—Gloria

Lord, it's a new day.
It's a new year, too,
      and a new decade,
          a new century,
              a new millennium.
There certainly has never been
      in my lifetime a better time
          to start something,
              become something,
                  do something new!
Yet as I step over the line
      into such a major moment in history,
          I bring the same old me.
I bring my old habits.
I bring my same old body
      with its same bumps and knocks
          and wrinkles.
I bring my same history
      and circle of relationships.
I bring my expectations
      of myself and others,
          both realistic and unrealistic.

Lord, *new* is easy to talk about,
    but it's hard to come by.
Only You can make me new.
And only You can help me keep and treasure
    what's old and precious.
Only You can show me
    what I should keep and treasure
        and what I should discard and change.
Lord, You are teaching me
    that Your work in my life
        is not a resolution but a process.
All things—good, bad—regular, exciting—
    joyful, painful—routine, innovative—
        all things work together
            to make me good,
                to make me what You want me to be.
Lord, it is easy for me to ask You
    to make me new this new year.
It is harder for me to ask You
    to make me consistent,
        enduring, patient, and submissive
            to what You're up to in my life.
But I do ask it.
Make me, Lord, the well-shaped vessel
    You're already molding
        with the tools of life—
            the very things I sometimes ignorantly pray
                that You will remove from my days.
This new year, I ask for trust and faith
    in what You're already doing in me.

Befuddled

They say that as people age, they often become becalmed, befuddled, bewildered—bewhat? They who? I suspect that the "they" is usually a bunch of someones who are younger than the people they are talking about. I suppose there are times I'd have to admit to such a description.

In this case, however, I'm not sure that age is the qualifying factor, since I've been a bit befuddled on this issue for a lot longer than I've been "old." It's about heaven—and whether or not there will be seaside beaches there.

In my mind, heaven has always been a seashore destination. In fact, a prerequisite for friendship with anyone in this thick and thin group is the intense desire never to be far from an ocean. We don't relate well to people who aren't happiest with sand between their toes and the stimulation of fresh salt air against their faces. For all four of us, even an hour by the sea effects the emptying of our cluttered minds and opens to us a kind of freedom—even a physical freedom. Bodies limp with prolonged pressures and exhausted by tensions are revived where the soul finds deep renewal in the romance of the sea's sound and motion. So naturally, we have assumed that since such revitalizing qualities are also those promised in the heavenly realm, there must, of course be an ocean in its geography.

But lately, I've been reading John's Revelation, and to my amazement (and befuddlement) there are several allusions to the fact that there will be no sea. The idea distressed me so that I rushed immediately to my big fat Bible commentary and began to research the situation. Well, as near as I can tell, the reason for no sea is that seas are dividers of people—and of course, you don't want a heaven with divisions. Hell is the place for such things! Dante had that all figured out long ago!

Now I haven't actually probed into the deep, underlying theological issues involved here, but I'm reasoning that surely a God who started out with such magnificent creations as tide pools and coral reefs and sand castles wouldn't end with just gold streets and pearly gates and ruby walls. Walls? Ooops! Don't walls divide? And in a place where it is always light, aren't gold streets likely to get hot? And then where will we all go to cool off? I'm confused. If the seas got to be an "in between" problem, it seems there could just be a supply of Mosaic wands made available to wave over the water. A nice, dry ride through the wave wall on a bejeweled chariot would be a thriller! Well, I'm not getting any definitive answers on the subject; I suppose I'll just have to wait and see. I've got to stop rambling on so. "They" may be listening; and I should be judged old and befuddled!

I Try Not to Look Too Surprised!

L ately I've been running into people I haven't seen for a long time. Women I have known in years past from my old neighborhood or with whom I served as room mother for one of my children during his grammar school days. I've noticed that I have to look twice to really recognize some of them, and they all seemed to have the same expression on their faces, an expression that could best be described as surprise or maybe shock!

I've thought to myself, *Boy! I must look older and more sickly than I thought! After all, this has been a pretty tough year.* But then it hit me! They weren't in shock from seeing me! That surprised look on their countenances came from their face-lifts! I must admit, stretching that skin as far as it can go does create a fresh look; more stunned than stunning, I think!

After this revelation, I went home feeling old and quite discouraged. I began to look at my face in the mirror. A fresh wrinkle appears nearly every day. The skin tone on the ole face is practically gone. Come to think of it, the entire body is sagging fast. Every part is moving south!

To top it all off (get it?), one of these days I'll have no trouble stuffing my bosom into the waistband of my slacks. As for the thighs . . . well, never mind! There are no words to express some things. Even the man who loved these thighs made derogatory remarks about them. Whenever he saw me preparing to eat a piece of pie, he'd quip, "Why not eat two pieces—one for each thigh?" What a smart mouth he was!

It is much too late for creams and anti-aging formulas. It's too expensive to go the health spa route, and it's too "not me" to go with a face-lift. Besides, I'm a big chicken. Having a face-lift now would be like putting braces on these big buckteeth of mine. Everyone says they are part of my character. I would hate for my own children not to recognize me.

I'm not sure I'd want to trade in my wrinkles for the "doe in the headlights" look! Each wrinkle is a story in itself. If they could talk, what a life they could record: pleasure and pain, ups and downs, good days and bad. The darkest of nights and the brightest of mornings. Pride and disappointment, terror and shock. In sickness and in health, for better or for worse, and even after death us did part! It's all there, written on my face and tucked away in my heart.

One of the characters in Pearl Buck's *The Good Earth* says of another character, "I don't really trust her, she is too smooth. I like 'em bumpy!" Boy, would she trust me. The bumps and lines, the cracks and crannies on this face have a story to tell, and I wear them all with pride. And I try very hard not to look too surprised!

Wrinkles Are a Mark of Character

My mother-in-law has one of those wonderful, craggy character faces—the kind you see in English films. She doesn't own a cosmetics bag because one is not needed for soap, water, and moisturizer.

I, on the other hand, do own a vast array of partially used, wrinkle-preventative solutions. Bob says if he had all the money I've rubbed into my skin, he could be a king. (But then maybe he'd have one great prune for his queen.) Maybe.

I've pretty much lost any hope for keeping up the facade of a fashionable body, but my face is one body part that has not suffered from lack of fitness training. I'm a smiler and a talker, and I meet surprise with visible exuberance. The china-doll look has never appealed to me. In fact, as an observer of dedicated early morning beach walkers, I have always greatly admired those spry, healthy looking seniors sprinting by. They are mostly leathery old ladies who look tough enough to chew on. Their faces speak of victory in both adversity and adventure. Long ago, I chose them over the blue hairs with perfect pink cheeks. There's just something about them that bespeaks spirit!

However, somewhere deep in my psyche, I have to admit I want it all—character, spirit, and smooth, lightly bronzed skin. My chances don't look good. The manufacturers of those "age-defying, line-diminishing" remedies mock the truth-in-advertising laws. They lack the integrity of a company like Sunsweet, whose claim for its prune problem is, "Today the pits . . . tomorrow the wrinkles." But when they finally achieve their goal, I want to be their first poster child. Okay, poster senior.

On second thought, I believe I'll just assume an alternative perspective. I'm siding with Victor Hugo, who said, "When grace is joined with wrinkles, it is adorable." Oh dear. Now I've got to start working on grace!

> I wouldn't swap one wrinkle of my face for all the elixirs of youth. All of these wrinkles represent a smile, a grimace of pain or disappointment . . . some part of being fully alive.
>
> —HELEN HAYES

I Admit It! I Think I Might Be Addicted to Metamucil

I don't know about Joy, Gloria, and Peg, but I've decided not to grow old gradually—or gracefully, for that matter. I'm an all or nothing type person, and I've never been characterized as graceful. Someday I'll just wake up and say, "Okay, this is the day; I'm old now."

Let's examine this question, look at both sides of the situation. Old can be very appealing. I'm talkin' verrrry appealing! Think about it.

Choosing to get old means you don't have to worry about how you look. Que sera, sera! No more hours at the beauty shop, dabbing at your smarting eyes; hey, let it go gray, girl; cut it off up to your eyebrows; get a curly perm! No more time sweating on the treadmill, unless of course you exercise for health reasons (I wouldn't know about that) as opposed to wanting to look like a sex siren.

Old means not having to worry about what you wear. "Yes, I realize I have on four long-sleeved sweaters at once. It's s'posed to turn cold. Besides, haven't you ever heard of—whoops, I must've dribbled there—layering?"

And think about it: no more panty hose! You can wear those knee-high things, or roll your stockings south to the ankles. Let go of the pain! And speaking of pain, you can go bra-less. You can tuck your boobs into your waistband if necessary. In case you think it's never been done, just ask Peggy!

When you are old you can say anything you please. Have you ever noticed that some people start talking old long before they get there? It's like they're testing it out. "I just worry about that parakeet of mine; I'd hate to think she'd outlive me. Who would clean up her messes?" I say, either get old—buy a rocking chair and a space heater—or euthanize the bird and quit worrying about it. And for heaven's sake, quit talking like you're eighty, saying everything that comes into your head. How you don't sleep well anymore when everybody knows you doze all day and your friends have seen your head roll practically off your shoulders during the sermon.

Then again, think how freeing it would be if you could say any old thing, complain about your aches and pains ad nauseam. And gas? You could exhaust (exhaust, get it?) that subject, talk about it for hours on end, and I don't mean the kind of gas you get at Texaco, either!

Choosing old means you don't have to think. I ask you, in some strange way, is this not appealing? Just to let your mind go? No more reading late into the night trying to keep up with Gloria. "I'm goin' to bed and watch TV." Doze and dribble, doze and dribble. As for Gloria, I'll just say it right out, "If it's not on television, I'll never know about it. What you don't know can't hurt you." Pretty soon Gloria would get frustrated and take you on as a project. She would start asking you questions about the past just to get your mind going, and with a blank look you'd say, "Gloria, I don't remember." Then she would come at you like a wildcat. With great indignation, she'd say, "What do you mean you don't remember?" Then everyone would be on your side and all over Gloria's case for badgering an old person. "She says she doesn't remember; now leave her alone," they'd say. "Go read Solzhenitsyn."

The other side of the coin is that to stay young, you have to be on your toes. When you really don't remember something and someone suggests you're losing it, you say, "Excuse me, but I have so much information in my brain computer that occasionally it takes me a moment longer to call it up than it would a younger person who has accumulated a third of the information I have."

Choosing to not be old means you have to have answers. "Well, of course I'm appalled at the political situation, and I intend to exercise my rights as a citizen. In fact, come next month, you'll find me in Washington lobbying on that very matter." It means you have to be up on technology. "A newspaper? You still read newspapers? I haven't dirtied my hands with those for years; you know how black your hands get, not to mention what they'll do to my new white sofa! (Even a reference to a new sofa implies you expect to live a while.) I get all my news from the internet! Have for years."

When I weigh the pros and cons of getting old, I realize I'm not there yet. I have standing appointments at Hair Villa and Nail World, and my wardrobe is fairly fashionable, if a bit gaudy. I'm still reading and keeping up with current events. And as to Gloria, although she's highly suspicious, she's yet to find out I get a lot of my information from *People* magazine. When it comes to technology, I've got that aced. I even have my own website: Suebue.com.

There is one thing that pulls me like a magnet toward the drip and drool side of the fence. Old people can behave pretty much as they please. If nothing else, on Sunday mornings I could sit at the end of the pew and pinch men's backsides when they scoot by. It would be so freeing. Someone would say, "Don't mind her. She's old!" Someone else would say, "You'll have to admit her row fills up in a hurry."

Just Like Laundry, Life Piles Up!

One of the best household jobs to save up for these grandmother days is ironing. I've always liked to iron and have taken a lot of ribbing from my children through the years for leaving the ironing board up just in case I get a few minutes to iron. Can't help it, I'm strange! But it fits right into being an on-call grandmother.

peggy

Take, for instance, the summer season, the time when I'm called on to be a full-fledged gran, a time when mothers and fathers, who were once my little angels, get desperate, crying on the phone and begging for my help with their little angels. All of a sudden, I become entertainer of the year to the little people in the Benson clan. Yesterday, after a two-day visit, I took my six-year-old granddaughter, Annie, home to her parents, and this morning at seven sharp, my son Patrick rang my doorbell and brought me his sleepy son, Luke, to spend the day and night with me.

Usually, they bring their own entertainment: toys, videos, CDs, games, puzzles, and books, not to mention sleeping bags, basketballs, and backpacks. (I may have to rent a storage space to keep their loot!) My job is to make conversation, provide a listening ear, and do meal and snack duty. It's "fun and games" for us all, but it is also a little hard on my concentration, so I am careful about how involved I get in my own work and life while the children are here.

I know that I might be needed at any minute to referee a dispute or to furnish a band-aid and a few kisses, so I don't try to balance my checkbook or pay the bills or do my income tax or write a book! I do what I did when my own children were small. I do something that involves cleaning or straightening, something that allows me to get a simple task done and at the same time keep one ear out for what the children are doing and give them a chance to "spread their wings." Ironing fits the bill for me! That large basket piled high with unironed clothes and the challenge of getting it done in a certain time period is somehow invigorating to me. (I know, I'm strange!) I like the idea of seeing stacks of freshly ironed clothing that only a few hours ago were in a great undone, unanswered pile, trying their best to get my attention. I can actually look and see proof of what I've accomplished, a job well done! So much of what women do must be done again in a day's time. It is nice to keep a stack of clean, pressed clothes on the shelf where I can see them and feel that well-done feeling. Besides, when Bob would come home and ask, "So what did you do today?" I could do the Vanna White thing, "Tada!" And he was quite impressed!

When I think back over the years of keeping house and raising children and all the hours I spent caring for my family, I am amazed I can still walk, much less think! I don't know how I managed. It makes me tired just to type a list of what I did back in the olden days when they were young. Cleaning, doing laundry, ironing, sewing, cooking, and gardening, not to mention errands, keeping dental and doctor appointments, going to church activities, taking trips to high school ball games. And did I mention school and nagging about homework? Boy, have I "been there and done that!" At the risk of sounding like June Cleaver, and as much as I love order, there is no way to put total order into the life of a family. Having a family is a matter of constant "rolling with the punches" and demonstrating the true meaning of the saying, "The best-laid plans of mice and men . . ."! Child rearing has reinforced my belief that women are truly the superior sex! Which may put us in danger of having a tacky, gaudy crown in heaven. A tad overjeweled!

Perhaps I'm going over the edge when I admit this, but I believe of all the household tasks I did, other than gardening, what I liked best was the simple task of ironing! I found it to be wonderful thinking and praying time, and unless there was a nose to wipe or a bloodcurdling scream from the playroom, I could use the time to talk things over with the Lord and let Him in on my thoughts and feelings. He has taught me the lessons of listening: if I am patient and wait and stay quiet, He will help me and encourage me and comfort me. Even as I do the mundane tasks of life. He gives me wisdom, and I take hope and come to realize once again that my large pile of out-of-control issues is safe . . . in His control!

I must say, at the end of the day, I wish the pieces of my life, like my laundry, were neatly pressed, folded, and stacked in complete order. But since I have a family and live in an imperfect world, I know the reality is that this is highly unlikely. In His wisdom, He sees fit to give me what I need and what is best day by day. I may never know a full season in which everything is neatly ordered, but the lesson here is to be true to the task and have faith that He is at work. I can trust Him, even when so much of my daily life refuses to be folded, pressed, or stacked the way I wish it to be.

> Now faith is being sure of what we hope for and certain of what we do not see.
>
> —Hebrews 11:1

Change Is Progress

Three Steps Forward, Two Steps Back

I sometimes exercise my wit by engaging myself in the pursuit of answers to profound intellectual questions. Doing so is, after all, one of the hallmarks of maturity. Recently, my cerebral ruminations have been concerned with the world of commerce. What has been happening in the buying and selling realm while I have been busy "maturing?" Everything seems to have gone change crazy, and at the speed of light. I'm not sure whether to be happy about it. I'm thinking it over. Aloud. On paper.

Of course I am only a very minute part of the grand commercial scheme, and I am seldom chosen as a participant in its opinion polls. Waning middle age is not the prime target area of most such investigations. But in the unlikely event that even one curious pollster should happen to pick up this book, I'm going to venture here a few passionate pieces of partisan sentiment. Though sure not to effect the reform of any major profit-making plans, they just might drum up enough sympathetic support to niggle the nation's conscience a bit. Okay, so this is just a random diatribe— one of those past-middle-age emotional spasms.

One of my pet peeves is that as soon as I locate an item of great comfort or satisfaction—such as a good brand of instant potatoes or a flavorful, nutty bread I love—"they" quit making it or decide to "improve" it.

I find a hairdresser who does the perfect cut, and he learns a "new technique." After buying and discarding hundreds of dollars' worth of discomfort, I at last seize on a bra that fits perfectly, and the next edition alters the strap to "better hide beneath the blouse"—a new, thinner (now with nylon-fortified lace) edge that digs into my shoulder!

Am I just off beat and out of step, or are the manufacturers too quickly bored? The commercial world has gone bananas. There is no longer any such thing as a bona fide B cup. What used to be labeled B now fits like an A+ or a B–. Is the "normal" American body now more high waisted and long legged than it used to be? In the case of underwear, I figure the designers are men who, minus the feminine instinct, just "don't get it," or they are women-haters who purposely design discomfort!

I remember when both sets of my five toes fit comfortably in a pair of shoes! The new styles are designed either to squeeze all the little piggies into a narrow, triangular configuration or let them hang indiscriminately out both front and back. The term *slide* is, however, an appropriate designation for the latter; one has to curl one's toes to keep the shoe from sliding off!

Please tell me why the new *haute couture* houses are using bad zippers (the kind that stick or split) and insist on putting them in places you can't reach anymore. T-shirts are too short-chested. Pants are manufactured in only two sizes—petites (too short) and regulars (too long). I'm a freak! Is God still making my size body? Somebody should tell Him . . .

And it's not only the apparel market that has gone awry. Birch beer—the kind we used to get at the boardwalk as kids—is now only bottled for and apparently exclusively distributed to *haute cuisine* cafes, those places that used to serve only imported wines and coffees. Has anyone else noticed that the single-dip ice cream cone has shrunk to the actual size of the dipper? And whatever happened to Junket?

It's almost impossible to buy a loaf of ordinary white bread. The shelves are amply stocked with thin, sandwich, diet, low-sodium, double crust, vitamin fortified, or the 50-percent-less-flour varieties. After much searching, I finally locate the next-to-the-last loaf of good, old-fashioned Wonder bread on a rather inaccessible top or bottom shelf.

Several years ago, I had the perfect hairspray. Not too gummy, not too stiff, not too wet. Didn't freeze my lungs when I inhaled. Didn't pull the teeth out of my comb the next morning. Just held my hair in place. Now the shelves are inundated with things like "movable" sculpting sprays. Who sculpts in hair? My old faithful has been discontinued and replaced by several soft-hold varieties. I just want a simple shot that will keep the hair out of my eyes. All day!

And this is just minutiae—the small change of change. What this all boils down to (old cliches are still in style and useful) is that few things in this world are forever. Okay, I admit that cling-ing to the familiar is a sign of dementia, but it can also be just good common sense.

Is progress always for the better? Yes, more people, more lug-gage, and, apparently, less food, can be carried on an airplane than used to be possible. More telephone calls can be received at the same time. In your own home, you can hang friends and telemar-keters on multiple call-waiting lines at once. Calls can be made from any point in the universe—not just those attached to wires. Several television shows can be viewed simultaneously on a single screen, and almost any kind of communication or information can be expedited by a computer-based network at any hour of the day or night, anywhere in the world. All in the name of progress. But progress toward what end?

More people with more mobility and more access to more information more quickly have also been responsible for the accel-eration and facilitation of catastrophe, criminal activity, and moral decay. Who profits? What do we gain as human beings? What is the eternal value in all of this?

The grand host of manufacturers, suppliers, and service organizations will hardly be affected when I drop from their charts into my six-foot earthen rectangle. The occasion may cause a microscopic blip on the actuary's spreadsheet at Prudential Insurance. If my wishes are posthumously observed by my children—old clothes, a cheap coffin, a modest, handmade monument of seashells, and a celebration service on the beach—the minimal activity will not stir any cockles in the cold heart of commerce.

In the meantime, I think I'm going to opt for a few things that change very little, and one that never changes. Compelling books, good art and music, tasty food, the great outdoors, the company of cherished friends and family . . . and God.

We Thought We Needed More Information

—Gloria

We thought we needed more information.
We thought that we would make better
  decisions if we knew more.
The apple offered control of our lives . . .
  of other lives.
If we just had the apple,
    our own personal apple,
      no one, not even God,
        could tell us what to do.
So we got the information;
    we drove at breakneck speed
      through the information highway.
We raced through the orchard
    making a network of brickyards
      between apple trees.
Now we have information.
We sit immobilized by so much information
    that we can no longer make choices—
We have no way to weigh so much information.
Dazed and intoxicated by the glut,
    we are paralyzed to act, to feel, to move.

The apple juice drips from our chins
    as we stare blankly
        at images of each other,
            images we can manipulate
                and alter on the screen.
Oh, Lord, we have too much information!
But we have lost—with our innocence—
    our wisdom,
        our outrage,
            our delight . . .
                our Eden.

Efficiency A+, Life Effect C−

I'm not a great skier. At best, I'm mediocre on blue trails, close to disastrous on black. I'm too old to be taking chances at breaking bones, but I'm willing to risk because I find nothing like skiing to clear my mind and free my spirit. The truth is that it takes such focus for me to move successfully from the top of the mountain to the bottom that any other concern I have in the world is temporarily wiped out. I love that!

Not long ago, in Colorado, I shared a lift with a gentleman who spent the entire ride up the mountain talking with his office on the cell phone. The conversation was so "business as usual" that I had to keep reminding myself that I was on a ski lift, rather than waiting in an airport gate area. It made me sad. I wavered between feeling sorry for the man and wanting to push him off the chair. Something was very wrong with that picture!

Ironically, in my normal habitat, I am a great champion of efficiency. My self-concept is strongly tied to my ability to accomplish more than one thing at a time. In fact, thinking back, I am somewhat surprised at my lack of admiration for my companion skier. I love making things happen quickly and effectively. It has become sort of a hobby of mine. Okay, so it screams obsessive-compulsive!

I think it all began in my teens when I worked spring weekends and summers as a long-distance telephone operator. It was back when operators sat at a switchboard, staring at a series of cords and holes that represented trunk lines to the major cities in Ma Bell's revered system. This was the "big time." Bell was the only telephone mogul in the country and by far the most efficient in the world. Why was no secret. When I picked up a signal and said, "Operator!" I was no *Laugh-In,* Lily Tomlin's Josephine type. I was the product of a rigorous training program that rewarded employees for being "top of the class" at juggling keyboard, cords, and buttons. The more calls an hour I could handle, the more valuable I became, the more money I made. I loved the challenge of becoming faster and better at handling complicated calls. I developed octopusian skills! No wonder I can't walk from the kitchen to the bedroom and back without taking a trainload both ways.

"Every member of the household needs to keep everything that belongs to him or her picked up every day." That directive was designed to save energy—mine! But it usually backfired. The kids usually rolled their eyes and pretended not to have heard. I spent more energy enforcing the practice than I would have spent picking up everything myself. More and more, in my mind, I became defined by how many balls I could keep in the air at once. It was a juggling act that I reasoned was necessary to run an orderly household, successfully fulfill the roles of wife and mother, daughter, sister, friend and neighbor, maintain a professional career in publishing and speaking, administrate children's programs at church, and be ready to entertain my husband's business associates on a moment's notice.

I enjoyed those years immensely, but I believed that they wouldn't have happened had I not been invested in keeping every plate spinning at the top of its pole. I actually kept a list of "Things I can do while talking on the telephone." How else does one keep a world like that in motion?

That was then. I was young and energetic and loved being the juggler. The world was only as complicated as I made it, and I was pretty much in control. Then I grew up, as did my world and our children. Suddenly there were more schedules to keep, more miles to cover, more problems to solve, more places to be at the same time, and the demands outnumbered the hours of my days. I began dropping a ball now and then, and finally I realized that I could no longer call upon that reserve energy to get to that last pole. The china started crashing down around me. "Simplify, simplify," I kept telling myself, but I couldn't even find time to pick up the balls and remove the poles. After all, I put most of this in motion. Surely, I could stop it, settle it, fix it. I just needed to make a list!

In the space of six months, another list rearranged my life drastically. I sold my shares and relinquished my active involvement in the publishing firm I had owned for twenty-five years. One daughter graduated from college and moved to the far side of the country. The other was involved in an accident in which her beloved horse died and she was seriously injured. We moved from the big, roomy house where we had lived for fifteen years to a smaller home in the country. My husband lost his business and suffered a stroke that marked the beginning of a serious failing of his health. I, of necessity, found myself applying for a job teaching high school English, and my body was making strong objection to all of the above. I went to bed for a few weeks. I couldn't get my head to think straight, and I was scared. I had never been on such a journey. I didn't know how to act. I had only ever practiced one response: snap out of it; get up and go on. So of course, I did.

The story would be much more compelling if I could say that I experienced some grand revelation or happened upon a magic book that zapped my spirit or gradually helped me sort out the broken pieces and begin to put things into perspective. But there was no efficiency expert who rushed in to list the casualties, reorder priorities, and set the future in motion. Rather, it was a slow, uncertain process of relinquishing control in exchange for trust and a new peace of mind.

Isaiah 26:3 makes it sound so simple: "You will keep in perfect peace him whose mind is steadfast, because he trusts in you." Just be in trust with the One who made you. I'm not as good at that as I'd like to be. I think it is significant that the verb is in present tense. His prescription for peace is not a promise about what will happen tomorrow. It's not about a future goal or destination. I'm so much better at keeping my eye on the goal (my list) than at just putting my heart in His trust and letting go.

Psalm 28:7 is the clincher: "The LORD is my strength and my shield; my heart trusts in him, and I am helped. [And here comes the delight of it . . .] My heart leaps for joy and I will give thanks to him in song."

Ending every day with a song of thanksgiving. Isn't that better than having the house straight and the lists neatly checked off?

These days, not everything gets put away in its place. Now that there are only the two of us, I pretty much pick up "everybody's" stuff. Even the bed sometimes goes unmade. And instead of being in a hurry to load the dishwasher, I have my morning coffee on the porch and linger to listen to the jays gossip about the ugly nest of a neighboring nuthatch.

Friendship is cherished. Life is less about doing and more about being.

So life at this stage is idyllic. Wrong. Inside this machine of flesh, there is still the will for neat and tidy and efficient, and many mornings, I awake with its motor already purring. It's just that there isn't enough fuel to keep it going! Life still has its discom-bobulated moments, but it is just a bit more likely to lay back of its own accord, take a deep breath, delight in the day God has made, and check the trust level.

Funny thing . . . skiing is one of the few activities in which the journey has always been more significant than the destination. Given my love for the sport and my English teacher affinity for metaphors, you'd think I'd have learned my lesson earlier. Nah!

Saying Good-Bye to Nantucket

Today is Friday. It's early morning, a lovely summer day on the island. Tomorrow is the day I leave this place I love so much. I go back to the mainland and to reality. In the words of Pooh Bear, "Oh bother!"

Maybe it's the Eeyore in me, but I always say good-bye when I leave because I might not get back again. This beach is one of God's finest creations. A place where I can find myself again. It may be the place the word *tranquility* was spoken into being! Through the years of my life, just knowing I can get back to the water's edge has kept me moving through the long days of winter. Life on an island seems to call for getting back to basics. I have especially found joy this week in sharing the simple pleasures with my friends.

Joy and I rode downtown in the Jeep this morning. We would prefer to walk, but because it is our turn to buy groceries for supper on the beach tonight, we decided to drive down and save our energy. Tonight's fare is hot dogs, chips, and Cokes. It will be topped off with the traditional campfire s'mores. Who could ask for more?

What a joy to come with friends to a place that holds such memories of times past. This is a perfect ending to a perfect week. Supper along the sand dunes on Dionis Beach. I am sure there will be sharing of favorite beach stories of times gone by. Some will recall memories of those who used to be with us at the beach. Those who have "gone home." There will be laughter as well as tears, and singing and tall tales and a celebration of the joy of being here together.

This bunch of friends has been through "the wars" together. Long ago, I think I realized that it is not what we know that holds us to each other but Who we know! I see the work of the Lord in these friends of mine. Some of them look better than others. (I won't call any names! They know who they are and aren't!) Some are smarter, some have more worldly goods, and some are younger. But all have one thing in common: a shared life in Him! I am thankful for being with people who show me by example "the way home."

Good-bye for now, Nantucket. In my dreams I visit you often, and through the lives of fellow travelers, I am reminded of where home really is! And I remember all those I love who wait on that heavenly shore for me. The day is coming when I will get to say hello! And I will hear their response, "Welcome home!"

One tiny selfish prayer: But Lord, if

you are listening and looking down over my shoulder . . . if you chose to route me "home" through Nantucket, I wouldn't mind seeing it one last time, not one little bit! Amen.

I am glad I am finally old enough to know that God might actually listen to a request like this!

Dedicated in loving memory to my faithful friend
Robert Roy MacKenzie,
a fellow seeker on the journey home.
We will see each other again
and spend time with the creator of waves!
Rest a while and look for me!

Lord, It Is Harvest Time

—Gloria

Lord, it is harvest time.
The ripe fields are being cut,
  their full grains carried
    by conveyors into waiting trucks,
      then driven off to storage bins.
Huge wagons loaded with baled grasses
  move like awkward prehistoric animals
    through the country roads,
      groaning with the weight
        of their burden.
Apples and pears, sweet and full,
  are sorted into wooden crates
    to be the central joy
      of craft festivals.
Root vegetables are being dug and hidden
  in dark cellars against the threat of winter.
Everywhere the reaping
  of fruit and grains and grasses
    celebrates the faithful work
      of spring planting
        and hot summer cultivation.
This, Lord, is the season to rejoice,
  the season to enjoy,

the season to rest from labor
and dance in streets and country roads
around warm bonfires.
I feel it in my bones, Lord.
I, too, am entering the season of harvest.
For so long I have wondered
what I would be when I grew up.
For so long I have done
as faithfully as I knew
just what the day demanded of me:
daily tasks, tending children,
meeting deadlines, passing out love,
finishing routines.
All of the while I felt as if one day
I would "turn out"—
do something special—be something
when I grew up.
Now, half a century of my days have passed
doing "regular" things the best I knew.
I smell the smoke of autumn fires
and feel the days shortening.
I hear the rustle of "gathering in."
I can see now that the daily *being*
was what I was to do.
Even now, my days are so "regular,"
my chores so unspectacular.
Yet I feel a festival in the air.
My grandchildren dance
in the leaves on the hillside.
My husband hurries home
to be warmed by hot soup

and a fire in the kitchen hearth
and our well-tested love.
My work has, on wings of its own,
    found its way into places
        I will never go,
    but joy has returned on the wind
        to sing at the festival.
Yes, this is harvest time.
    The fruit is ripe and sweet.
Help me, Lord,
    to see the life You've given me
        in a new and joyful perspective.
Help me to embrace the process of seasons.
May the harvest bonfires
    be a sweet incense
        to Your nostrils, too.

Just Old Enough to Know

I am more myself on a good day in the classroom than at any other moment in my life. Teaching is both my calling and my joy. My family would attest to my inability not to teach, which of course they often see as to their detriment.

But it is good to have arrived at this place in life and have in my store of treasures the deep satisfaction of having been in exactly the time and place for which I was purposed. It is even lovelier to have lived long enough to have gained the insight with which to recognize the pleasure of this discovery.

Such a discovery is not unlike the contentment felt each time you slip your feet into your most comfortable old pair of shoes or nestle into a pillow that cradles your head and shoulder perfectly or experience a hand clasp so friendly and perfect (the right size, pressure, texture) that you never want to let go. It is a moment of rightness that you just know is sure and trustworthy; no rationale, no explanation, is needed. It is simply that you are seasoned enough, loved enough, tough enough, have lived long enough to know!

I've Stopped Looking for That Perfect Age

(In Fact, I Think I May Have Missed It)

When I was six, I wanted to be ten. A ten-year-old got to stay up late, cross the street by herself, wear whatever she wanted, and have a friend over to spend the night.

When I was ten, I wanted to be sixteen. Oh, the life of a sixteen-year-old! Definitely the perfect time of life, if for no other reason than being able to drive a car!

Somehow being sixteen wasn't quite it, but I was certain being old enough to go to college was.

Surprise! Surprise! It wasn't! All college girls talked about was wanting to get to the next stage of life. Married. Oh, how we wanted to get married! Now that would really be it!

On and on it went, this search for it. You get married and that's good, but there's this nagging feeling that something is missing. Oh yes! Kids! Everyone else is having children, so real fulfillment must come with having kids. Absolutely! Positively!

You have a baby, and after a year or so you realize two would be better. Maybe three. Then one day you're sitting in a car-pool line, trying to figure out how you'll get Molly across town for her dance lesson and Matthew back across town to his soccer game. Frozen groceries are melting in the back seat because you didn't have time to go home and unload between shopping and driving the field trip for the fifth-graders. You have an epiphany! *It* is when the kids are old enough to fend for themselves. No wait, even better! *It* is when they get through school, move out, and can really fend for themselves . . . and duh!—why didn't you think of it sooner?—the financial burdens are over!

But then the kids are gone, fending for themselves—although never quite, because you're still sending checks. You're working as hard as you ever did. Maybe harder. And with less energy! At last you realize: there just ain't no such thing as it. "I may as well just add a couple of letters to *it* and call it *quit*," you say.

"Eureka! That's it!" you say. "Quit is it! What am I waiting for? Retirement, here I come." So you pack it up, have a garage sale, sell the house, move to a condo in Sunshine City, and buy white furniture.

"Yes sir, this is it. Hey, Frank, is this it or what? Frank, are you listening to me? Frank! Wake up. Frank! Get your grubby feet off that white furniture!"

After a couple of months of it, you notice Frank is getting hard of hearing, or at best has developed selective hearing. As for you, you've spent so much time in the Jacuzzi, you remind yourself of a raisin mass that's been in the refrigerator way past its prime. You are beginning to look like Mother Teresa. Yes, she was a holy lady—I don't mean to be disrespectful—but you'd have to be blind not to notice her skin tone! I'd be willing to bet my new sixty-dollar jar of rejuvenating cream from L'Oreal that not only wasn't she into rejuvenating but she never used moisturizer a day in her life, much less one with SPF-15.

Not only do you stop looking at yourself in the mirror but you begin to talk to yourself, ask yourself questions. Telling questions. If this is it, why am I comparing myself to Mother T and avoiding mirrors? If retirement is all it's cracked up to be, why does my back go out more than I do? Why is it that when I bend down to pick up my shoes, I find myself checking to see if there are other things I can do while I'm down there?

You realize the only reason you don't sin is because you don't have the urges you once had, that all the names in your little black book end with M.D. Worst of all, you plan your whole week around church . . . and enema night!

Eeek! I don't like to think about it. So right now, while I'm in my right mind (no comment from my three friends, please!), I think I'll sit down and reevaluate. Won't you join me? Let's rethink our priorities, then do our best to live and enjoy each day to the fullest. Maybe I'll even do something I swore I'd never do: put up those tacky little plaques that say such things as, "Live today like there is no tomorrow," or, "This is the first day of the rest of your life." Perhaps I'll stock up on music that causes my spirits to soar and hang out with people who know how to celebrate life, people who don't pull me down but build me up.

Yesterday is history; we can't change it no matter how much we'd like. Tomorrow? Who knows? It may be better or it may be worse. This is it. This day. This hour. This moment. The decision is mine as to how it will be spent. Perhaps being a little more like Mother Teresa would be good.

We Have This Moment, Today

—Gloria

Hold tight to the sound
  of the music of living—
Happy songs from the laughter
  of children at play;
Hold my hand as we run
  through the sweet, fragrant meadows,
Making mem'ries of what was today.

For we have this moment
  to hold in our hands,
And to touch as it slips
  through our fingers like sand;
Yesterday's gone,
  and tomorrow may never come,
But we have this moment, today!

Tiny voice that I hear
  is my little girl calling
For Mommy to hear
  just what she has to say;
And my little son
  running there down the hillside,
May never be quite like today.

Tender words, gentle touch,
   and a good cup of coffee,
And someone that loves me
   and wants me to stay;
Hold them near while they're here,
   and don't wait for tomorrow
To look back and wish for today.

Take the blue of the sky
   and the green of the forest,
The gold and the brown
   of the freshly mown hay,
Add the pale shades of spring
   and the circus of autumn,
And weave you a lovely today.

For we have this moment
   to hold in our hands,
And to touch as it slips
   through our fingers like sand;
Yesterday's gone,
   and tomorrow may never come,
But we have this moment, today!

Losing Is Better Than Winning

In one of my old journals, I found a quote by Nellie Hershel Tullis that I had once thought worthy of note: "The next best thing to winning is losing. At least you've been in the race." I suppose lots of people have entertained that thought, and at first rereading, I too responded from the amen corner. Finishing the race is often more important than winning; commitment is the thing—knowing you've tried, been true to yourself, fought to reach the goal, kept the faith, etc. Upon reconsideration, however, experience teaches us that sometimes losing is better than winning.

Of course, the natural, sin-scarred woman in me doesn't want to acknowledge that; I hate losses. I see them as frustrating setbacks, a sort of deity-instigated disciplinary measure that I resent. I find myself muttering to God under my breath (so as to soften the offense, in case He gets impatient with such meddling in His business), "Okay, Lord, I've been a bona-fide adult the better part of my life now. I'm old enough to know that after the dying and dormant seasons, new life always springs forth. The dawn follows the darkness, the sun'll come out tomorrow—guaranteed. So you don't have to keep reminding me. You don't have to keep proving yourself. I've got it!"

Now the redeemed soul in this same woman looks back at those times of adversity and recognizes the immense blessing that always accompanies the suffering and sorrow. There in the losing places is the profound enrichment of meaningful relationships. The restoration, renewal, and reconfirmation of friendship. The surprise support of a brother or sister you had no idea was journeying with you as an advocate, a yoke bearer. Losing often forces sudden passage to places of spiritual rehabilitation where we are confronted with the arrogance of self-reliance and learn lessons of dependence.

I am struck by Haddon Robinson's meditation on a verse from Psalm 51, recounted by my favorite devotional writer, Ken Gire, in his book, *Reflections on the Word*. It was a true story about the practice of shepherds who discover in their flock an errant sheep—one who, night after night, wanders from the fold. After many such meanderings and recoveries, the shepherd breaks a leg of the sheep, then keeps the miscreant close by his side as it heals. Hopefully the sheep learns the lesson that the shepherd represents his safety and security and henceforth stays near to the shepherd. I'm sure, to the sheep, the process seems coldhearted and punitive, but that is only because he "does not understand the heart of the shepherd." The broken leg is meant to cause not misery but restoration.

How many times on my journey I have thought myself broken by calamity, unsuspecting that the moment was part of a masterful plan to bring me back to my senses—to truth I already knew. Even now, in spite of the continuing joys and successes of my journey so far, I am at a stage in life where I am often persuaded that I have passed the pinnacle of my physical, emotional, intellectual energy. I have peaked! I am on my way down! The crest of the wave I have long enjoyed riding is now threatening to trounce me to the bottom of its whorl and deposit me naked and gasping on the beach. As crazy as I am about the beach, that is not a pretty picture!

At this losing place, a peculiar opposite and positive reaction materializes. I am also aware of a growth spurt and the resurgence of my learning curve. At this place in life where my hopes and dreams meet with the reality of declining years, I am in the process of becoming more real. Oh yes, I am less confident, but I am far more content.

How like God to break the leg of his errant sheep, love her to pieces, then let her wash up, of all places, on a beach—slightly battered but utterly at peace.

Okay . . . so it's a mixed metaphor! I'm not *only* an English teacher. Language proprieties be hanged!

Let me hear joy and gladness;
Let the bones you have crushed rejoice.

—PSALM 51:8

Growing Together

I t was nearing the last of October when I went to the bottom of the hill with a basket and two of my grandchildren to see if there were any late-ripening tomatoes. I had left the three wandering plants in the corner of my flower garden because we had not yet had a killing frost, and I hated to lose one single vine-ripened Indiana tomato if it could be rescued.

gloria

"There's one!" cheered Lee as he dove beneath the tangled mat of entwined foliage and came up with a lopsided but firm red tomato. Before we were done, we found six in all, as well as several pointed red peppers and a couple of small eggplants. (I have a habit of mixing a few vegetable plants among my flowers in the spring when I add the annuals to the faithful perennials.)

This outrageously glorious fall day, the chrysanthemums were bragging to each other,

arguing over which of them was the greatest in the floral king-
dom—the hot yellows and vibrant rusts or the deep burgundies
and the mauvy pinks. I refused to cast a partisan vote and picked
handfuls of them all to take to the house. Madeleine was filling her
little hands with mums too when we noticed what we called "the
last rose of summer"—a soft pale pink beauty whose petals were
edged in deep rose. It was then I spotted a huge pure white iris in
full bloom. Three more full buds lined its stalk.

"Look at this!" I shouted with enough amazement in my voice
to draw both Lee and Madeleine to my side. "What, Mamaw?
What did you find?" asked Lee, always eager for an adventure.

"Irises just don't bloom in October," I marveled as I cut the
healthy stem, "and for that matter, neither do roses, usually." We
added those rare treasures to our basket and started back up the
hillside.

Three of the seasons blooming together, I thought—spring, summer, and fall, all dancing together in the golden October sunshine.
That's what heaven will be: all the joy and none of the pain, all the
glory with none of the restrictions. Buds, flowers, fruit, and seeds
will be on one tree at the same time. All the fragrance and anticipation of spring, all the full joy of summer, all the reward of harvest, all the rest and peace of winter—these will fill the timeless
hours.

I thought of the thrill of insight, the excitement of revelation,
the adventure of discovery. There, in heaven, the breakthrough to
what is true will never cease. Wave after wave of "knowing face to
face" will leave us shaky with excitement. And we will never see
the end of such discoveries but will, at the same time, be "filled
up with God himself" (Eph. 3:19 LB).

I was reminded of friends and family I had known here and
"lost." Time and perspective have caused the history of them to
merge into one moment. My mother, for instance, died at eighty-
four of liver cancer. At the end, she was unable to communicate in
the brilliant, witty way I had known to be her trademark. Yet now,
six years later, those last few weeks had been pushed far into the
background and what was emerging was simply "mother." Mother,

young and adventuresome; mother, wise and deep; mother, funny and mischievous; mother, serious and insightful; mother, intellectual and hungry to know; mother, curious and childlike. All of what and who she was through my whole lifetime blended, now, into "mother." The total had not erased the specifics of her; indeed, the "completed" image seemed to intensify every little detail, amplifying every characteristic that was her.

I am coming to believe that heaven will reveal those we love in their total "perfected" uniqueness. There we will see each other as God now sees us, and we will be only beautiful—His perfect bride, the delight of His heart. Just as our surroundings will be an ever-expanding total joy, so will those who share this place be a kaleidoscope of crystal facets at which this life could only hint.

Just as all the seasons will dance there together, so will humor, tenderness, patience, loyalty, intelligence, serenity, and surprise dance in the eyes and souls of all we meet. We will all be a song; we will all sing our days. God Himself will be the perfect tone to which we all will tune, and harmony will be the unstoppable result.

Green grass and snow, flowers and fruit, summer and winter, springtime and harvest, wondering and knowing, profound worship and unrestrained laughter, youth and wisdom, outrageous joy and deep serenity: all these are heaven. There, there will be no end, for love will have outlived faith, hope, and the law (1 Corinthians 13).

And oh, yes. Today I noticed that the tall new growth on the lilac bush by the driveway had sprouted into fragrant blossoms. I put those blossoms in my kitchen window to remind me . . .

Acknowledgments

"Give Them All to Jesus." Phil Johnson and Bob Benson Sr. © 1975 Multisongs—a division of Careers–BMG Music Publishing, Inc. (SESAC). All rights reserved. Used by permission.

"I Will Go On." Words by Gloria Gaither. Music by William J. and Gloria Gaither. Copyright © 1979 William J. Gaither, Inc. All rights controlled by Gaither Copyright Management. Used by permission.

"The Servant Song" by Richard Gillard. © 1977 Scripture In Song (a division of Integrity Music, Inc.)/ASCAP. All rights reserved. International copyright secured. Used by permission. c/o Integrity Music, Inc., 1000 Cody Road, Mobile, AL 36695.

"Someone Is Praying for You." Words and Music by Lanny Wolfe. Copyright © 1977 Lanny Wolfe Music. All rights controlled by Gaither Copyright Management. Used by permission.

"We Have This Moment, Today." Words by Gloria Gaither. Music by William J. Gaither. Copyright © 1975 William J. Gaither, Inc. All rights controlled by Gaither Copyright Management. Used by permission.

FRIENDS THROUGH
THICK AND THIN

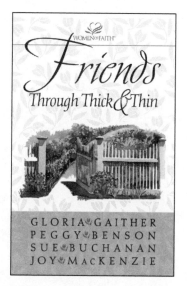

GLORIA GAITHER • PEGGY BENSON
SUE BUCHANAN • JOY MACKENZIE

Gloria Gaither, Peggy Benson, Sue Buchanan, and Joy MacKenzie have been friends for over thirty years. In *Friends Through Thick and Thin*, they celebrate the ups and downs and all-arounds of friendship: how they've cheered each other on in good times, supported each other in hard times, and shared heartaches, fun, and laughter through it all. Join them for an intimate, down-to-earth look at the secrets of lasting friendship.

Using the metaphor of nurturing a garden, Gloria, Peggy, Sue, and Joy offer insights into creating a healing, helping, and humorous circle of friends. Preparing the soil, planting the seeds of friendship, enjoying the bloom of friendship . . . the women share the lessons they've learned about cultivating relationships that grow stronger and more beautiful through life's seasons. From the funny, to the tragic, to the poignant, to the refreshingly frank, each short chapter is a slice of life.

Friends Through Thick and Thin is an upbeat, encouraging look at the relationships that enrich our lives. It's a wise, wacky, and honest glimpse at things that will help you nurture the garden of your own friendships. And it's a joyous, personal time of sharing with four extraordinary women.

Hardcover 0-310-21726-1

Softcover 0-310-22913-8

Pick up a copy today at your favorite bookstore!

ZondervanPublishingHouse
Grand Rapids, Michigan

A Division of HarperCollinsPublishers